FIRST 50
LOVE BALLA

YOU SHOULD PLAY ON PIANO

T0083076

ISBN 978-1-70516-500-3

HAL•LEONARD®

Visit Hal Leonard Online at
www.halleonard.com

World headquarters, contact:
Hal Leonard
7777 West Bluemound Road
Milwaukee, WI 53213
Email: info@halleonard.com

In Europe, contact:
Hal Leonard Europe Limited
42 Wigmore Street
Marylebone, London, W1U 2RN
Email: info@halleonardeurope.com

In Australia, contact:
Hal Leonard Australia Pty. Ltd.
4 Lentara Court
Cheltenham, Victoria, 3192 Australia
Email: info@halleonard.com.au

CONTENTS

6   Against All Odds
    (Take a Look at Me Now)

3   All By Myself

14 All I Know

18 And I Love You So

22 Because You Loved Me

11 Can You Feel the Love Tonight

30 Can't Help Falling in Love

27 Don't Know Much

35 Every Breath You Take

40 Fire and Rain

44 A Groovy Kind of Love

48 Have I Told You Lately

52 Hopelessly Devoted to You

32 How Long Will I Love You

56 How Will I Know

60 I Get to Love You

66 I Just Can't Stop Loving You

72 I Only Have Eyes for You

76 I Say a Little Prayer

80 I Will Always Love You

69 I'll Be There

82 I'll Have to Say I Love You in a Song

90 I'll Never Love This Way Again

85 I'll Stand by You

94 I'm Yours

100 It Had to Be You

112 Just Give Me a Reason

105 Love Me Like You Do

118 My Girl

126 My Heart Will Go On
    (Love Theme from 'Titanic')

132 Need You Now

136 Sea of Love

140 She Will Be Loved

146 She's Always a Woman

123 Signed, Sealed, Delivered I'm Yours

154 Someone Like You

162 Still the One

151 Strangers in the Night

166 Thinking Out Loud

172 A Thousand Years

178 True Love Ways

180 Unconditionally

186 The Way You Look Tonight

190 When You Say Nothing at All

197 With or Without You

202 You Are the Reason

194 You Are the Sunshine of My Life

210 You Had Me from Hello

215 You Make My Dreams

220 Your Song

ALL BY MYSELF

Music by SERGEI RACHMANINOFF
Words and Additional Music by ERIC CARMEN

Lyrics:

When I was young, Livin' a-lone,

I nev-er need-ed an-y-one, I think of all the friends I've known,

and mak-in' love was just for fun. but when I dial the tel-e-phone,

Those days are gone. no-bod-y's home.

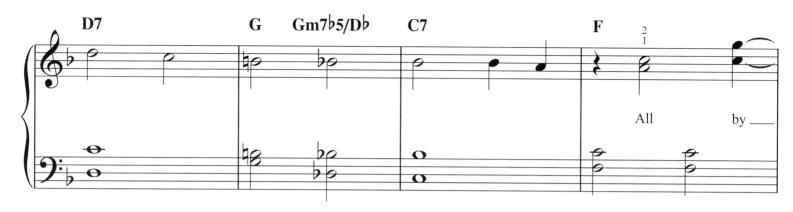

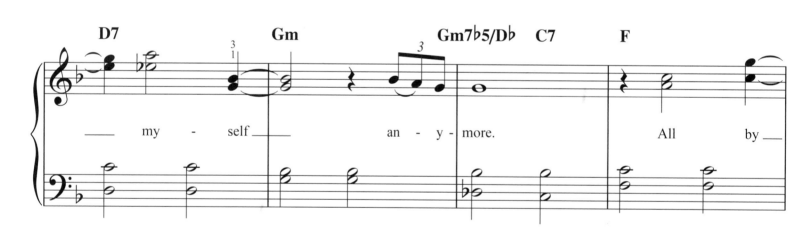

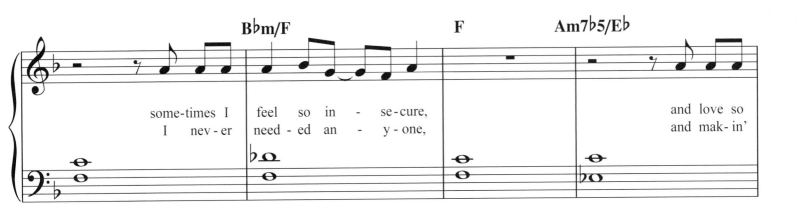

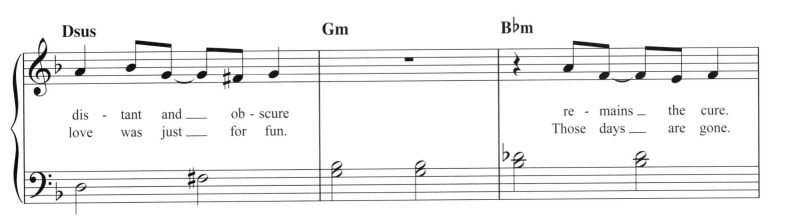

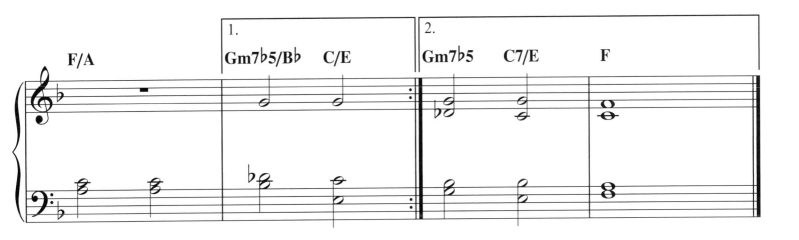

AGAINST ALL ODDS
(Take a Look at Me Now)
from AGAINST ALL ODDS

Words and Music by
PHIL COLLINS

Slow Rock

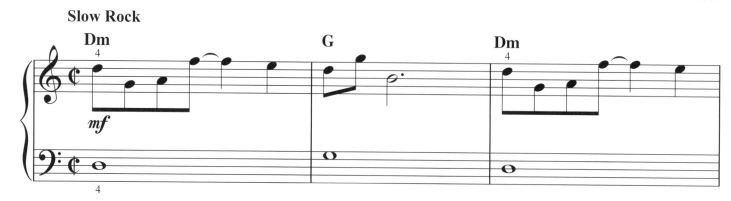

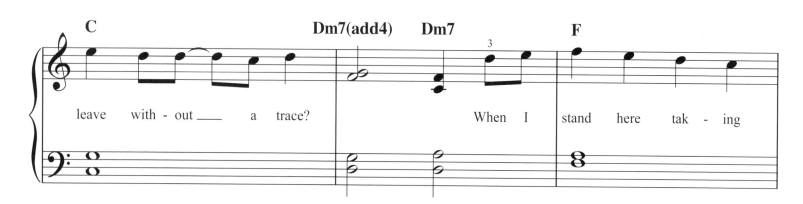

1. How can I just let___ you walk a - way, just let you
2.,3. *(See additional lyrics)*

leave with - out___ a trace? When I stand here tak - ing

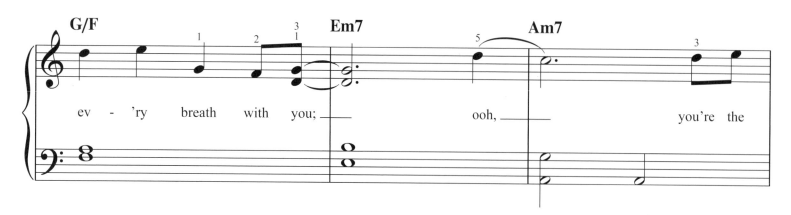

ev - 'ry breath with you; ___ ooh, ___ you're the

on - ly one who real - ly knew me ___ at all. ___

Chorus

So take a look at me now, ___

well, there's just an emp - ty space. ___

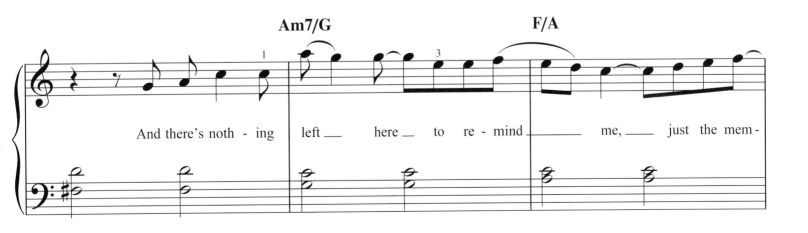

And there's noth - ing left ___ here ___ to re - mind ___ me, ___ just the mem-

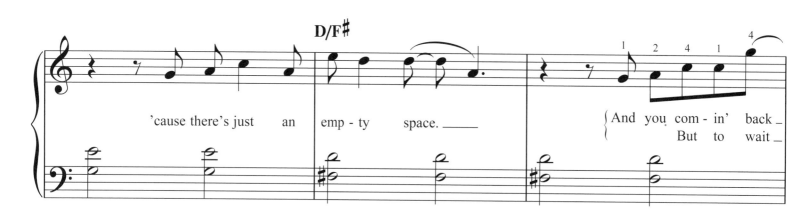

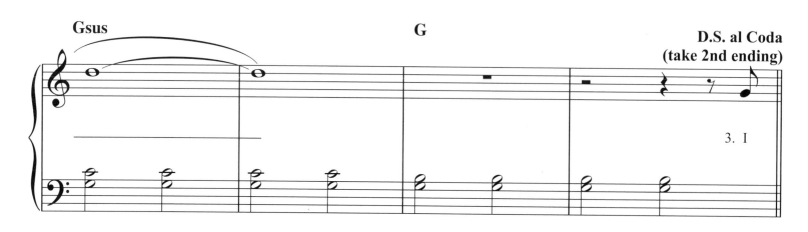

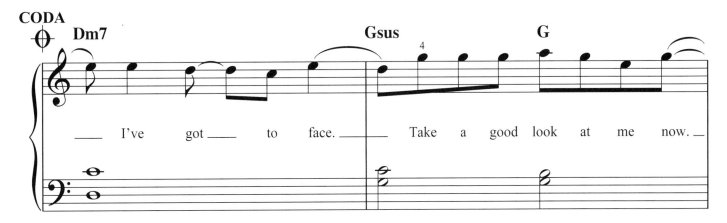

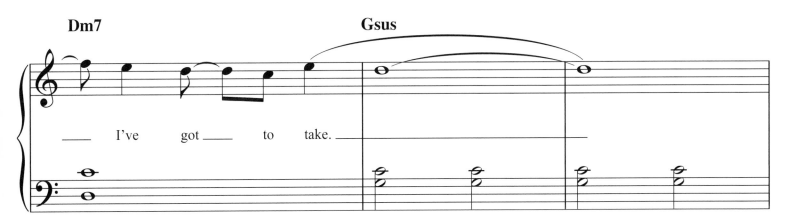

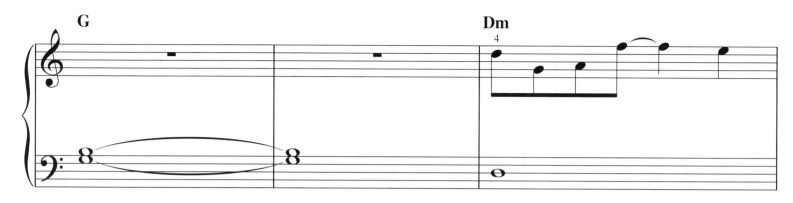

Take a look at me now. _

Additional Lyrics

2. How can you just walk away from me,
   When all I can do is watch you leave?
   'Cause we shared the laughter and the pain,
   We even shared the tears.
   You're the only one who really knew me at all.
   Chorus

3. I wish I could just make you turn around,
   Turn around and see me cryin',
   There's so much I need to say to you,
   So many reasons why.
   You're the only one who really knew me at all.
   Chorus

CAN YOU FEEL THE LOVE TONIGHT

from THE LION KING

Music by ELTON JOHN
Lyrics by TIM RICE

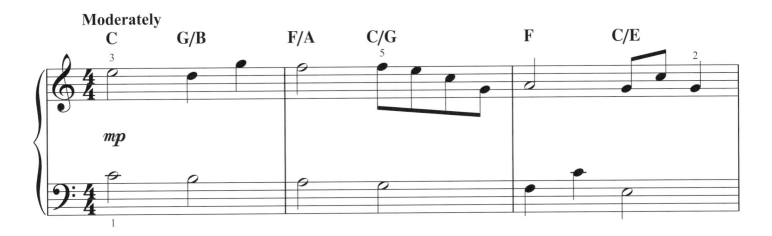

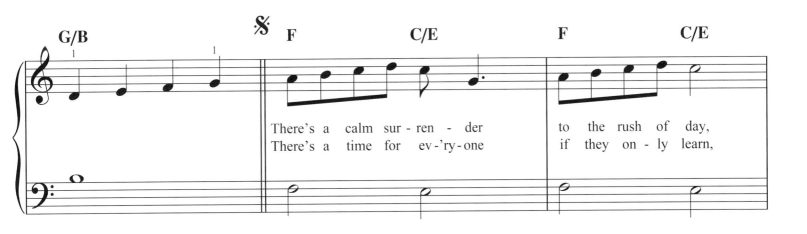

There's a calm sur-ren-der   to the rush of day,
There's a time for ev-'ry-one   if they on-ly learn,

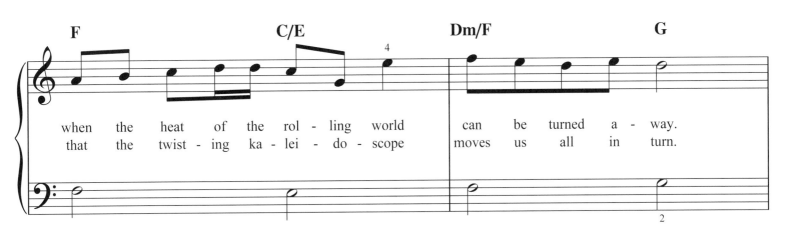

when the heat of the rol-ling world   can be turned a-way.
that the twist-ing ka-lei-do-scope   moves us all in turn.

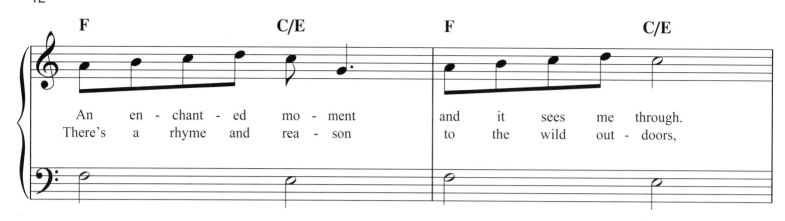

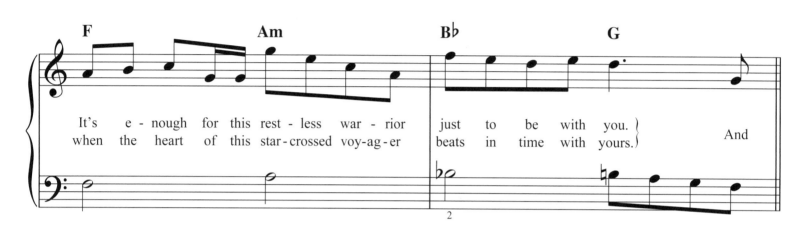

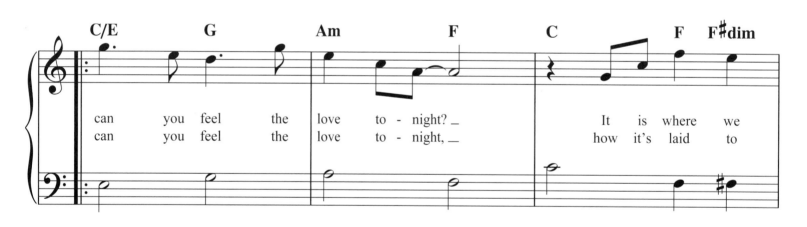

that we got this far. And lieve the ver - y best. __

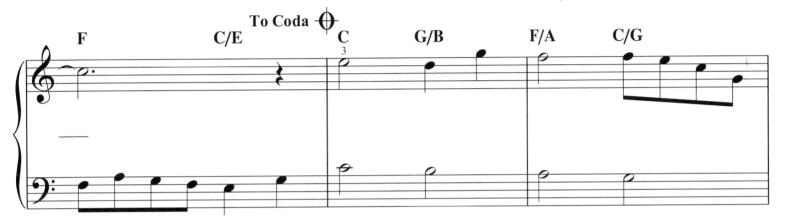

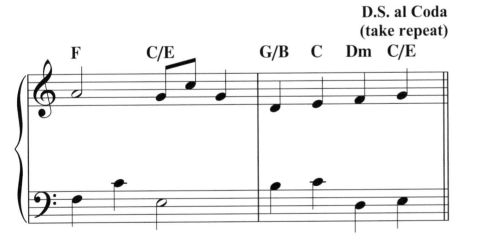

It's e - nough to make

kings and vag - a - bonds be - lieve the ver - y best. __

rit. e dim.

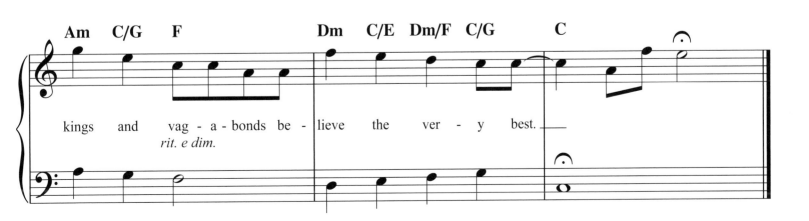

ALL I KNOW

Words and Music by
JIMMY WEBB

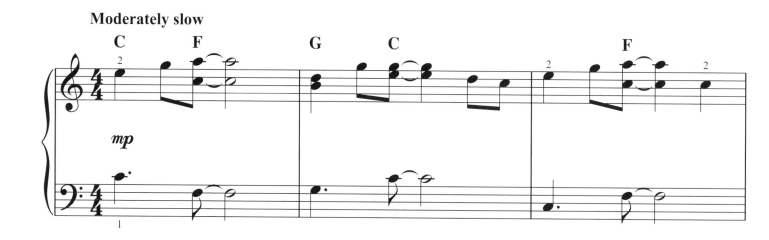

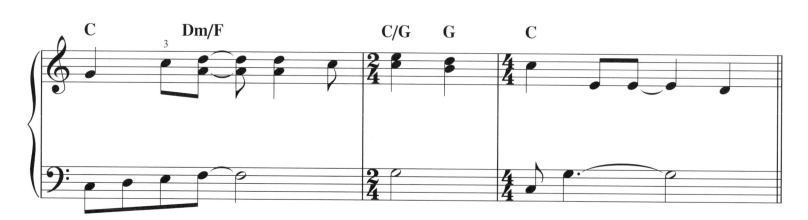

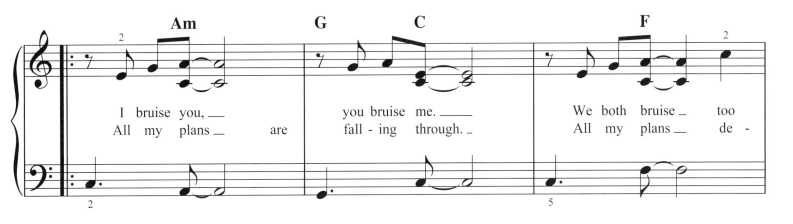

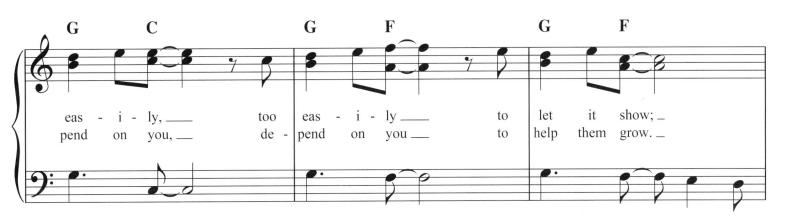

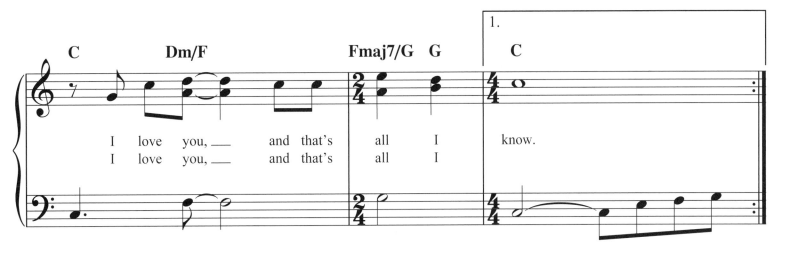

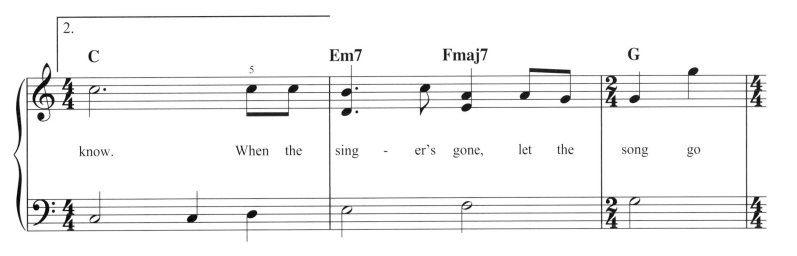

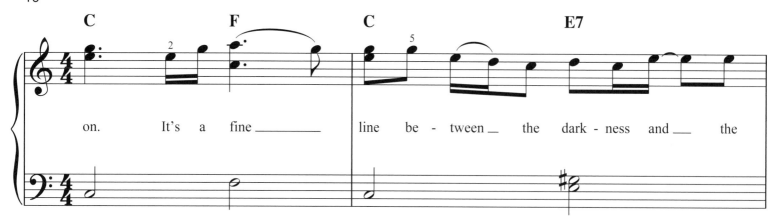

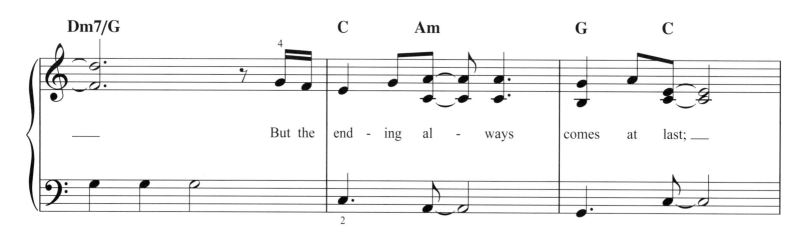

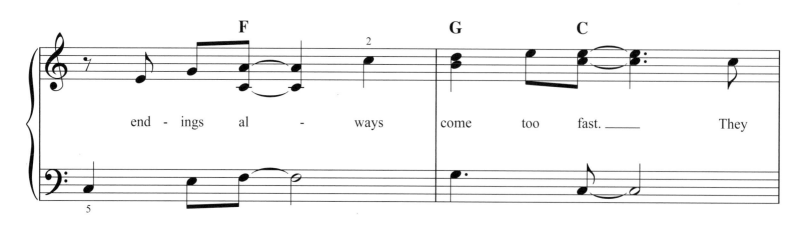

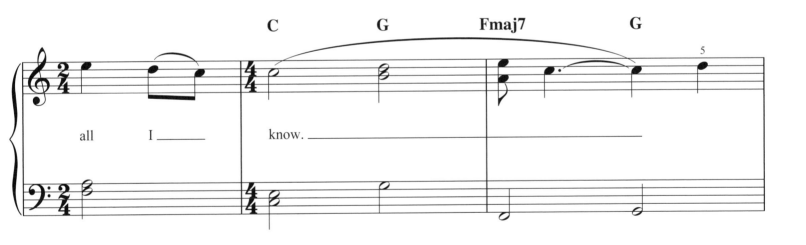

AND I LOVE YOU SO

Words and Music by
DON McLEAN

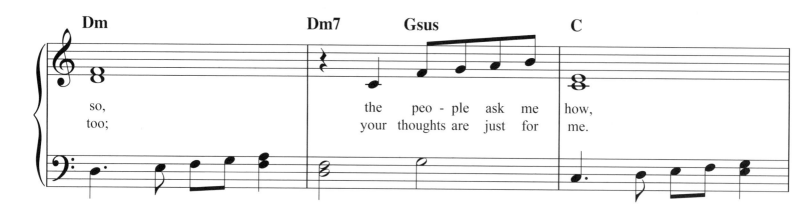

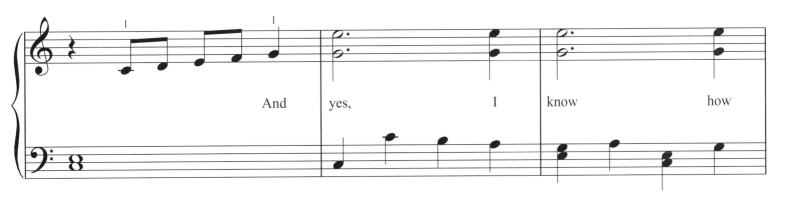

me and the night won't set me free. _____ But

I don't let the eve - ning get me

down, now _____ that you're a - round

me. _____ me. _____

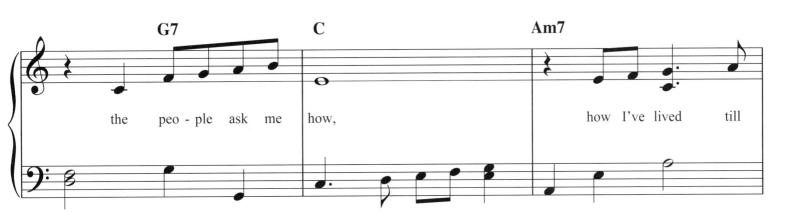

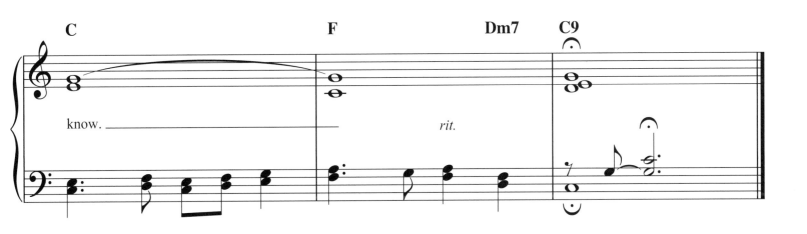

BECAUSE YOU LOVED ME

Words and Music by
DIANE WARREN

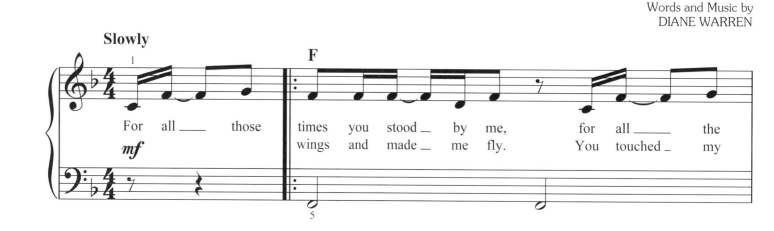

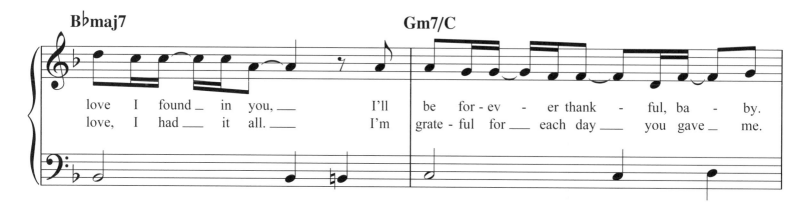

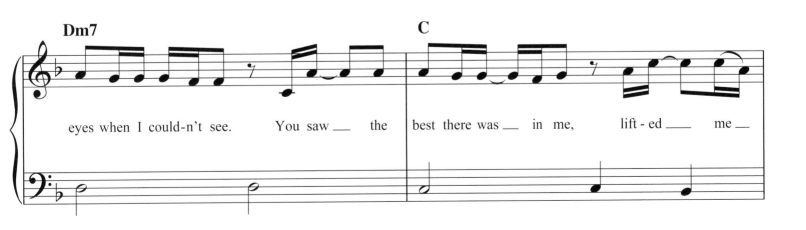

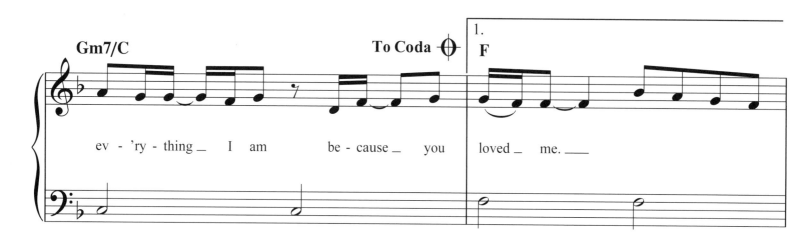

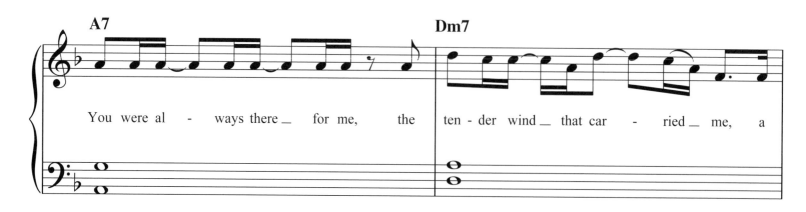

light in the dark, __ shin-ing your love __ in - to my __ life. _____ You've

been my in - spi - ra - tion. _____ Through the lies, __ you were __ the truth. My

world is a bet - ter place be - cause __ of you. __ You were __ my

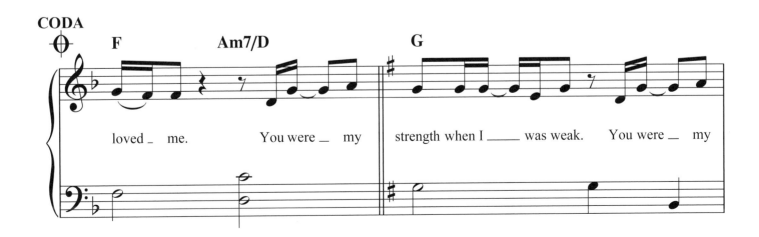

loved __ me. You were __ my strength when I _____ was weak. You were __ my

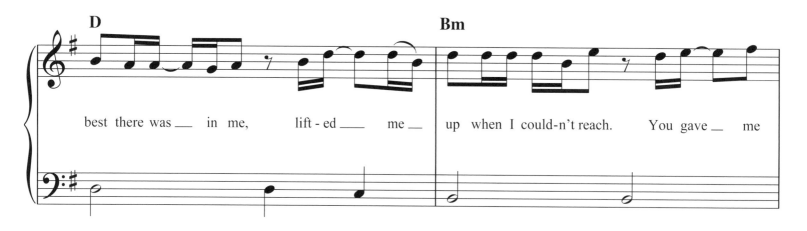

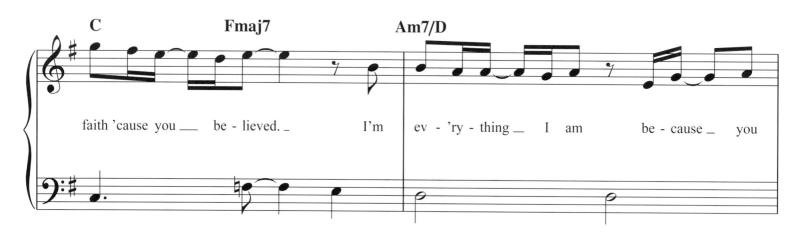

DON'T KNOW MUCH

Words and Music by BARRY MANN,
CYNTHIA WEIL and TOM SNOW

29

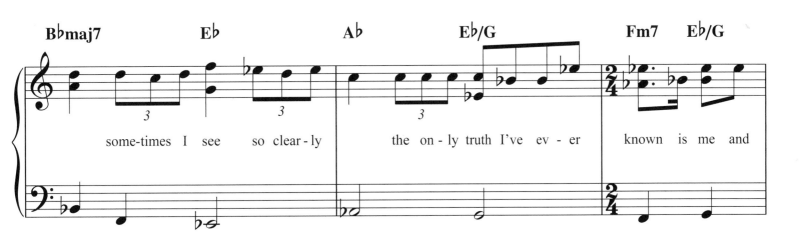

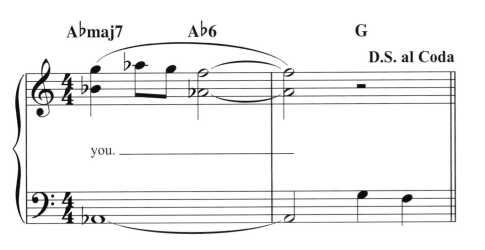

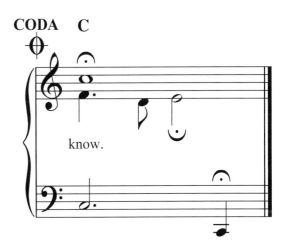

CAN'T HELP FALLING IN LOVE

from the Paramount Picture BLUE HAWAII

Words and Music by GEORGE DAVID WEISS,
HUGO PERETTI and LUIGI CREATORE

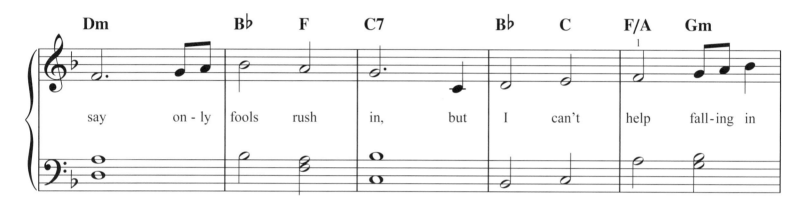

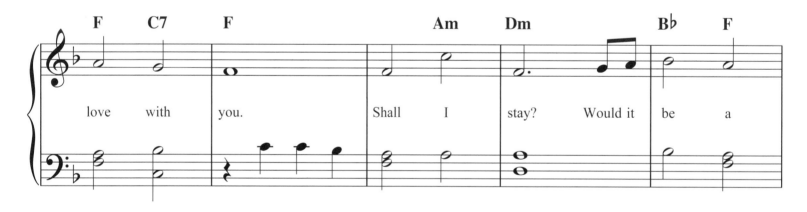

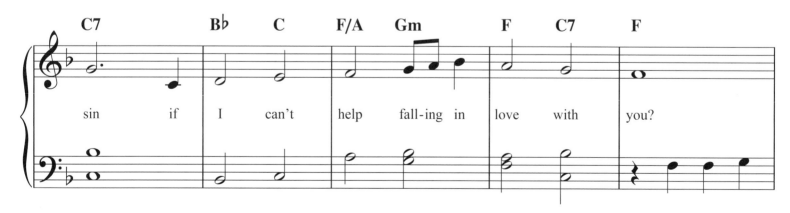

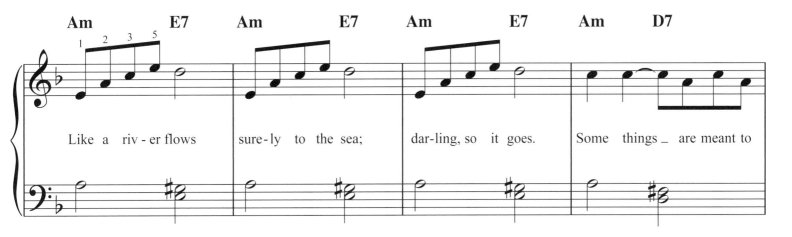

Like a riv-er flows | sure-ly to the sea; | dar-ling, so it goes. | Some things _ are meant to

be. | Take my | hand, take my | whole life | too. For

I can't | help fall-ing in | love with | you. For

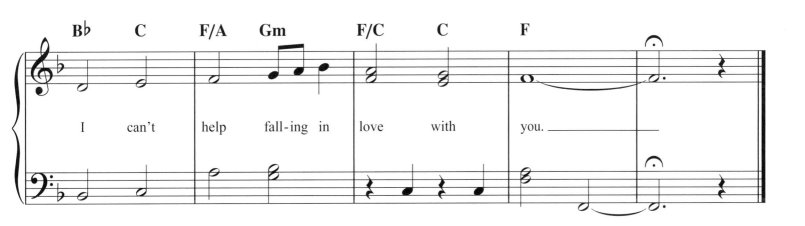

I can't | help fall-ing in | love with | you. _

HOW LONG WILL I LOVE YOU

Words and Music by
MIKE SCOTT

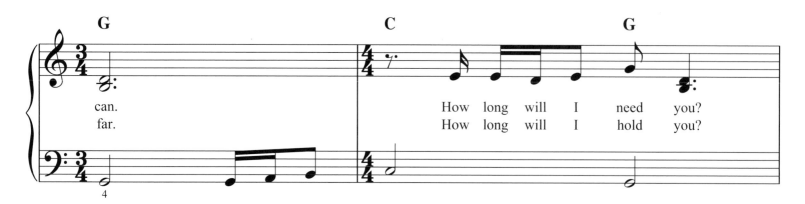

say. _____

How long will I love you?

As long as the stars are a-bove you, _____ and long-er if I

may.

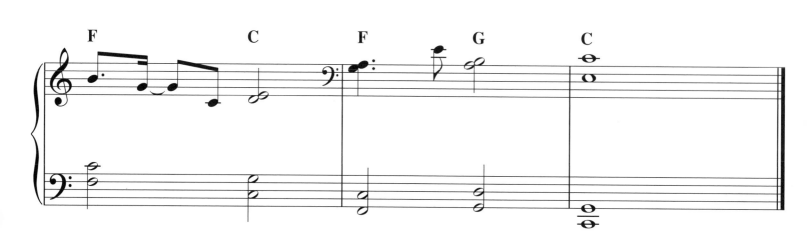

EVERY BREATH YOU TAKE

Music and Lyrics by
STING

Ev - 'ry breath you __ take, __ ev - 'ry move you __

make, ev - 'ry bond you break, ev - 'ry step you take,

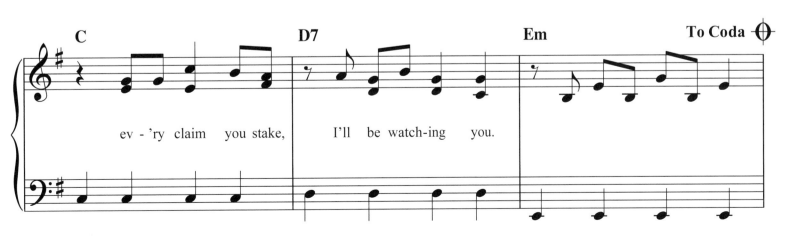

FIRE AND RAIN

Words and Music by
JAMES TAYLOR

I've seen fire and I've seen rain. I've seen

sun - ny days __ that I thought would nev - er end. __ I've seen

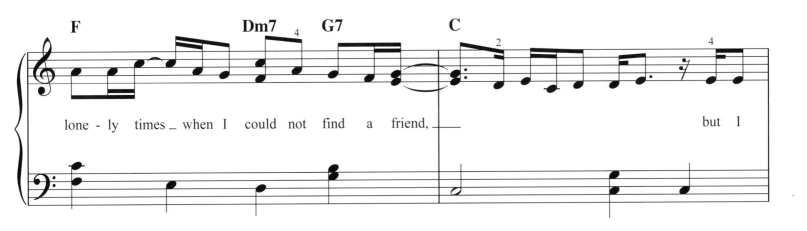

lone - ly times __ when I could not find a friend, __ but I

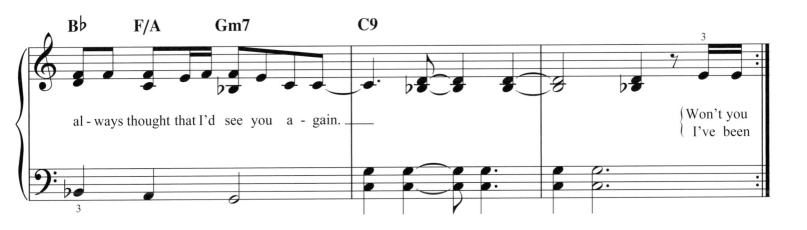

al - ways thought that I'd see you a - gain. __ { Won't you I've been

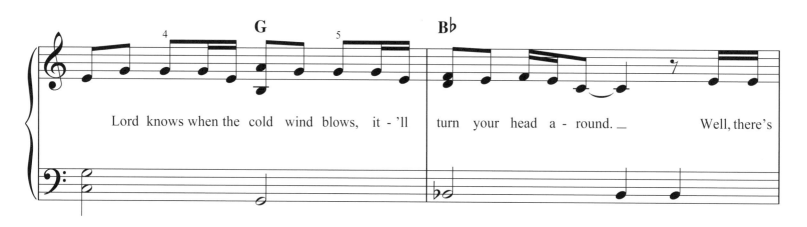

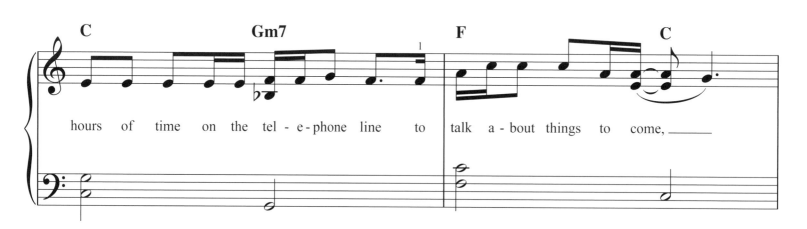

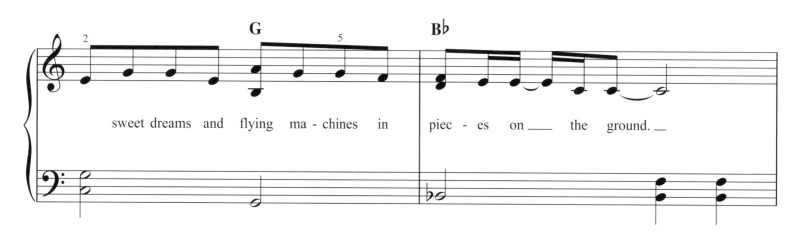

I've seen fire and I've seen rain. I've seen

sun - ny days __ that I thought would nev - er end. __ I've seen

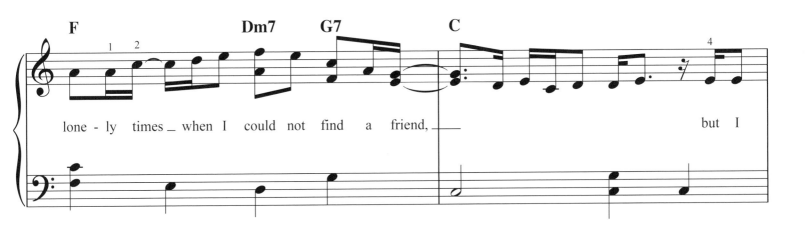

lone - ly times __ when I could not find a friend, __ but I

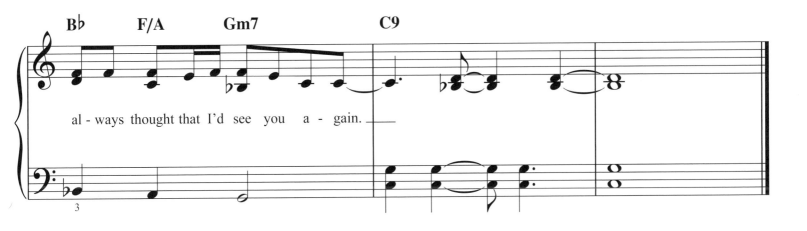

al - ways thought that I'd see you a - gain. __

A GROOVY KIND OF LOVE

Words and Music by TONI WINE
and CAROLE BAYER SAGER

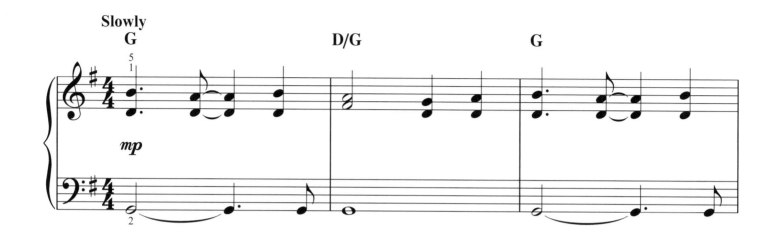

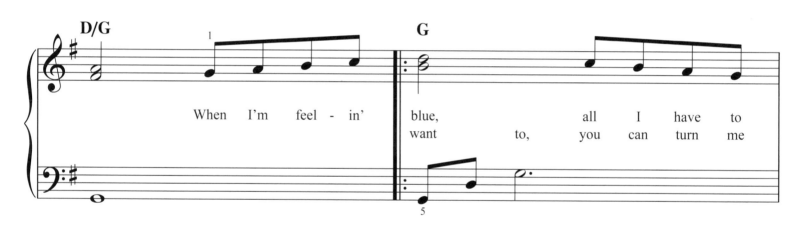

When I'm feel-in' blue, all I have to
want to, you can turn me

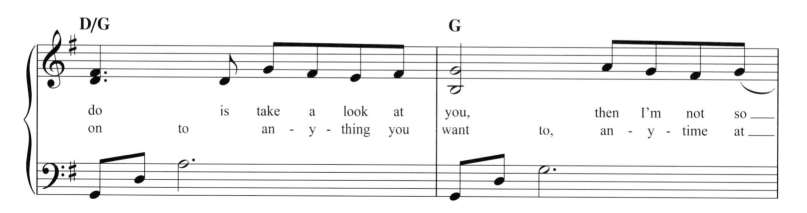

do is take a look at you, then I'm not so ___
on to an-y-thing you want to, an-y-time at ___

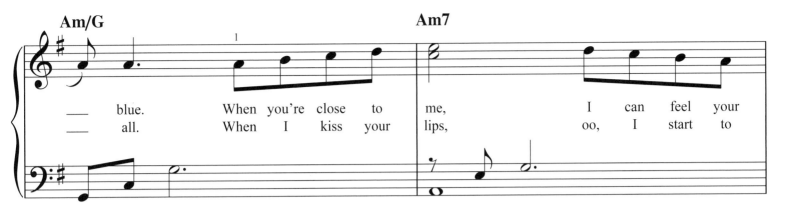

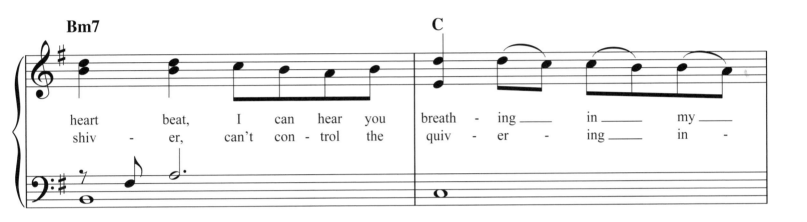

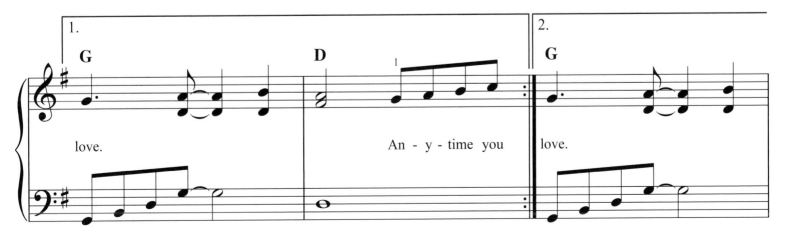

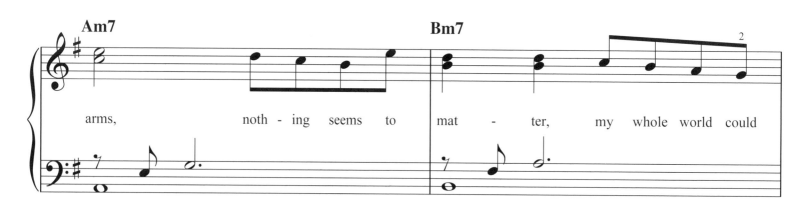

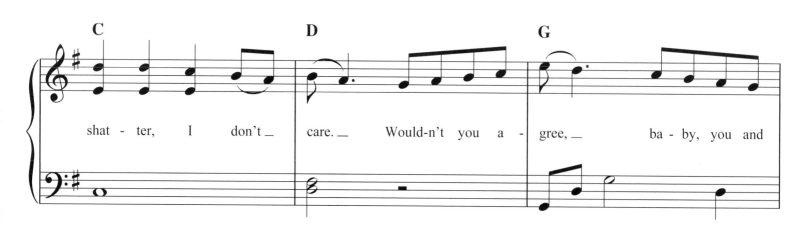

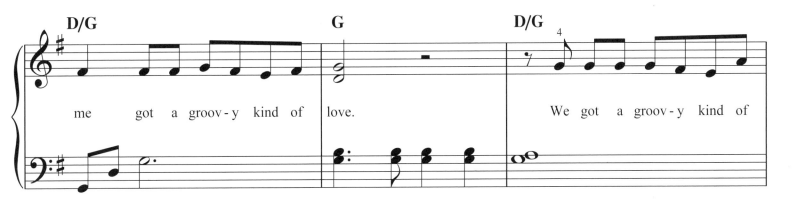

me got a groov-y kind of love. We got a groov-y kind of

love. We got a groov-y kind of love.

We got a groov-y kind of love.

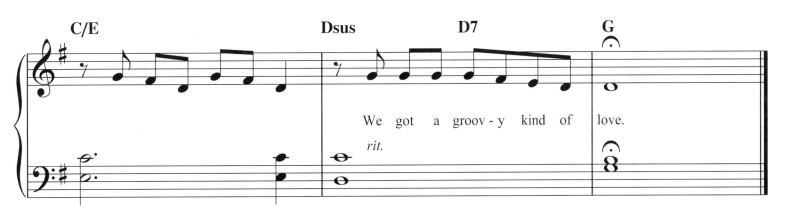

We got a groov-y kind of love.

rit.

HAVE I TOLD YOU LATELY

Words and Music by
VAN MORRISON

Slowly, with expression

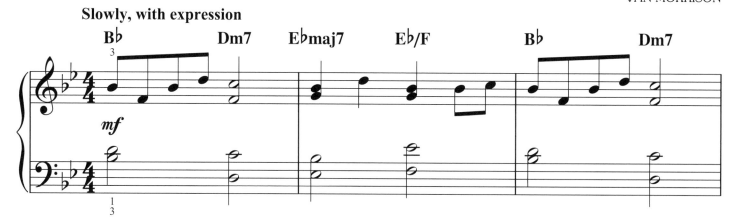

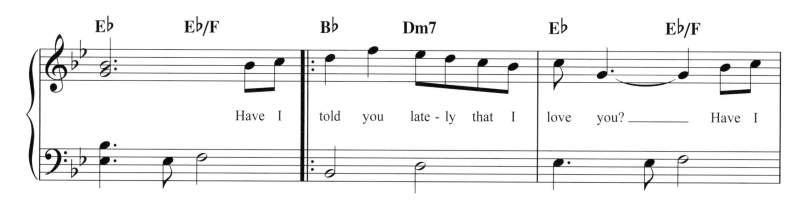

Have I told you late-ly that I love you? _____ Have I

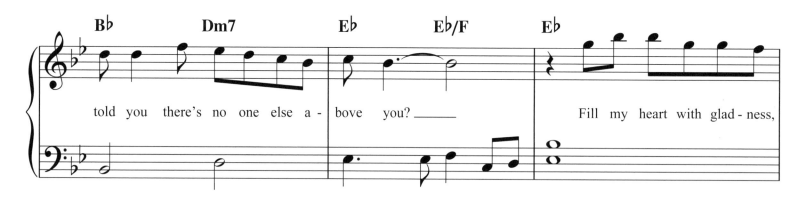

told you there's no one else a-bove you? _____ Fill my heart with glad-ness,

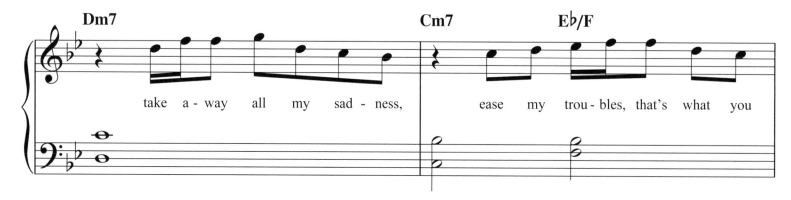

take a-way all my sad-ness, ease my trou-bles, that's what you

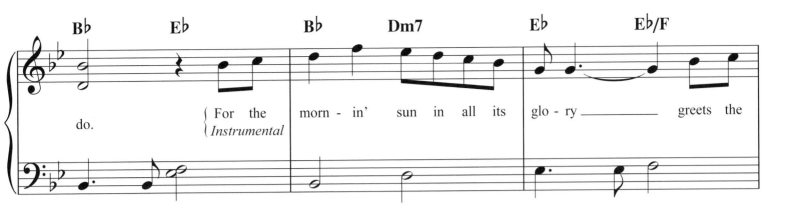

do.

{ For the
Instrumental

morn-in' sun in all its glo-ry _____ greets the

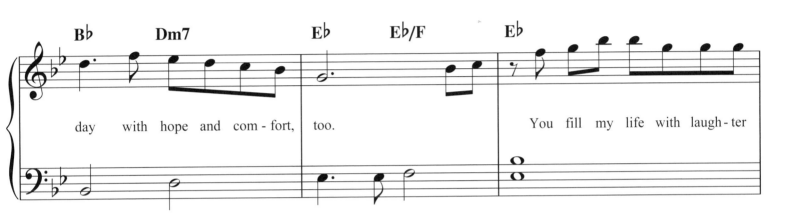

day with hope and com-fort, too.

You fill my life with laugh-ter

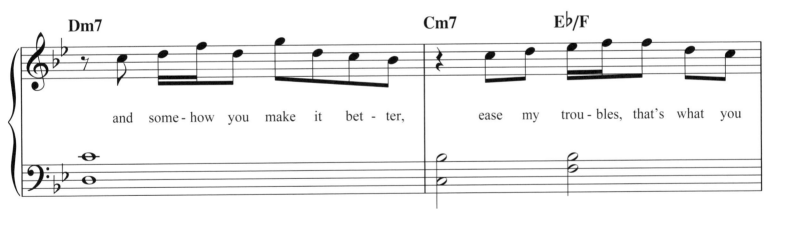

and some-how you make it bet-ter,

ease my trou-bles, that's what you

do.
Instrumental ends }

There's a love that's di-vine

and it's yours and it's mine _____

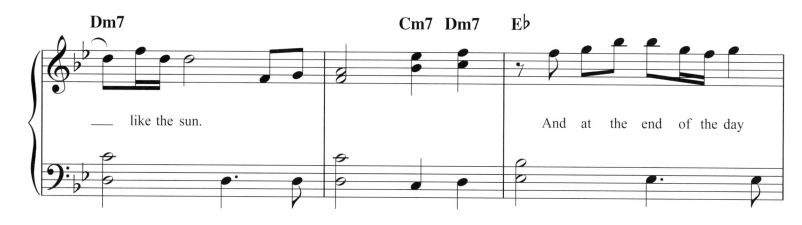

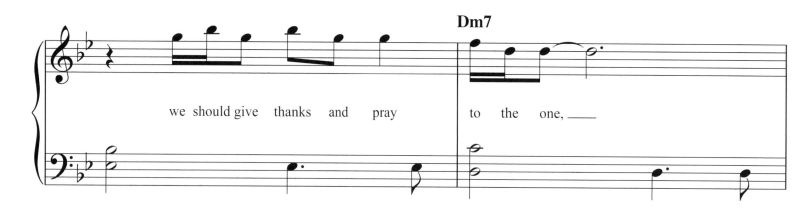

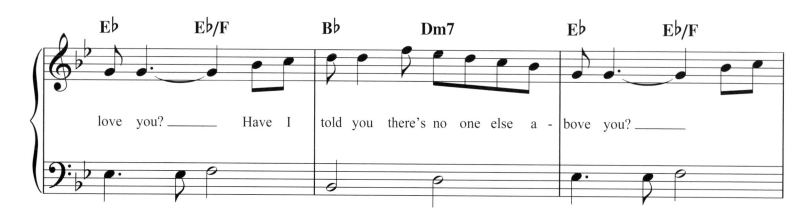

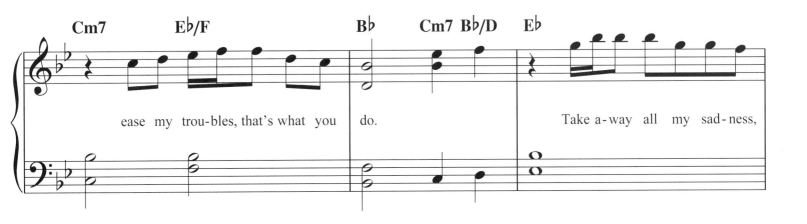

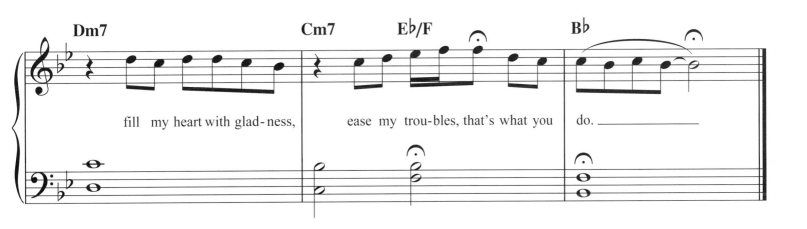

HOPELESSLY DEVOTED TO YOU
from GREASE

Words and Music by
JOHN FARRAR

Moderately, in 2

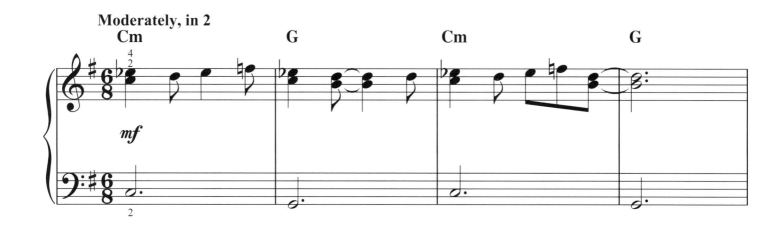

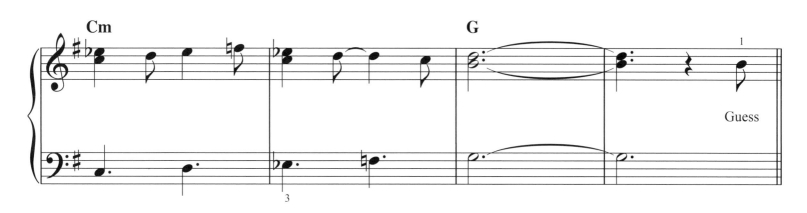

Guess

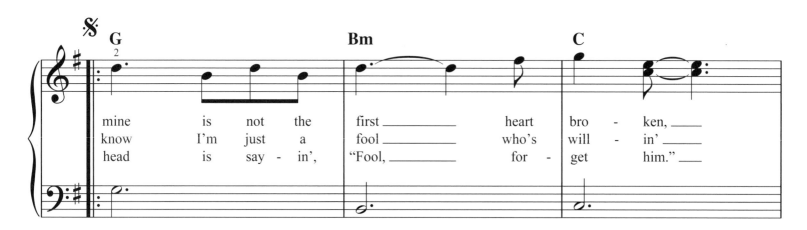

mine	is	not	the	first _____	heart	bro - ken, _____
know	I'm	just	a	fool _____	who's	will - in' _____
head	is	say - in',	"Fool, _____	for -	get	him." _____

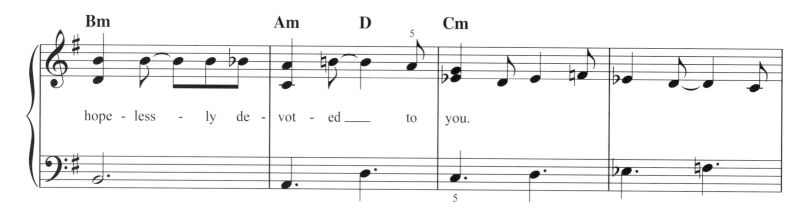

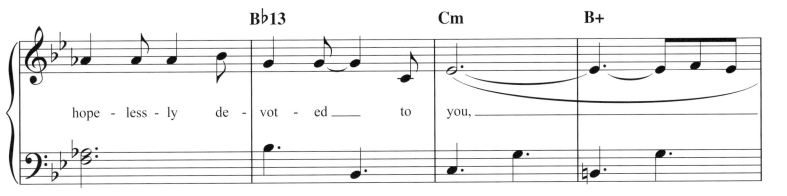

hope - less - ly de - vot - ed ____ to you, _____

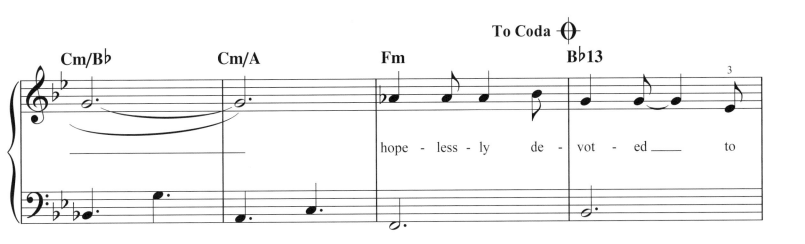

____ hope - less - ly de - vot - ed ____ to

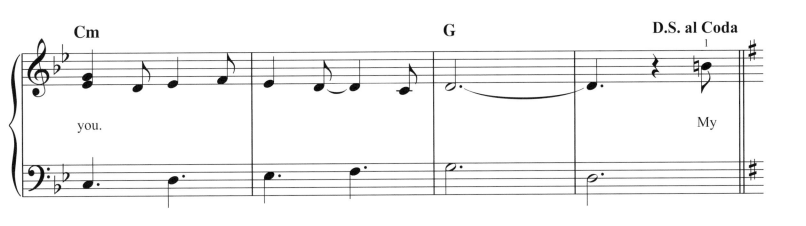

you. My

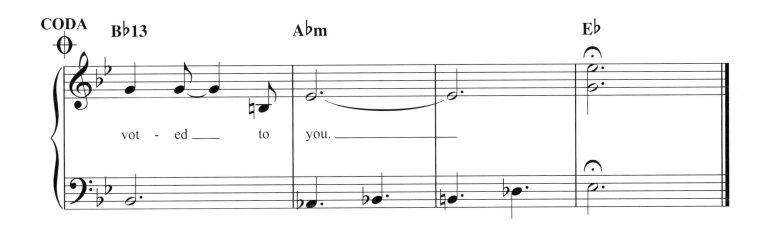

vot - ed ____ to you. _____

HOW WILL I KNOW

Words and Music by GEORGE MERRILL,
SHANNON RUBICAM and NARADA MICHAEL WALDEN

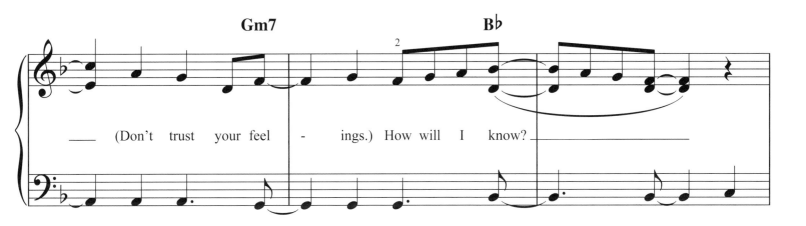

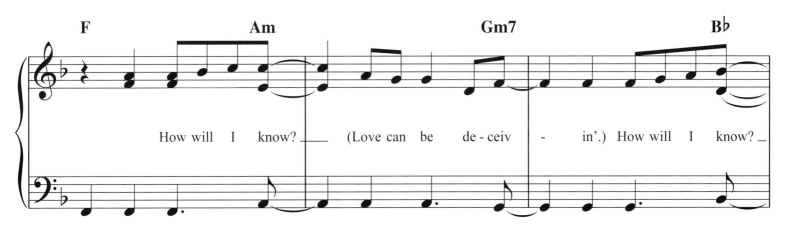

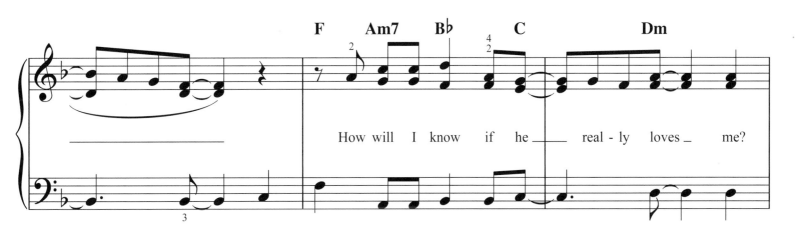

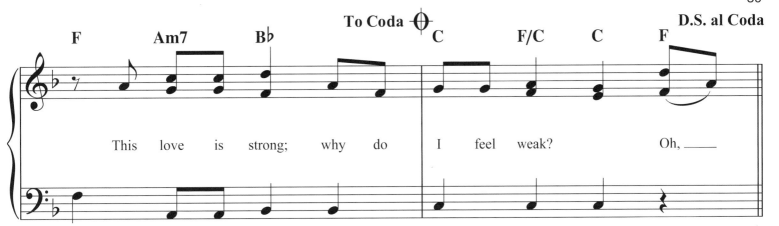

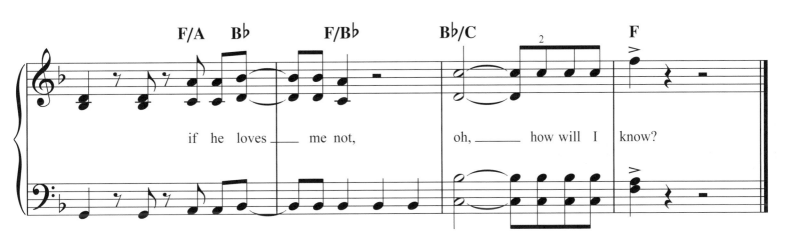

I GET TO LOVE YOU

Words and Music by MAGGIE ECKFORD
and MATT BRONLEEWE

Gently, in a slow 2

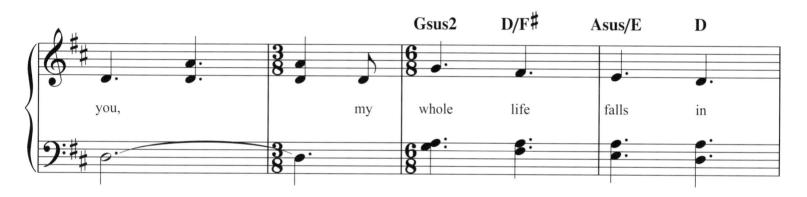

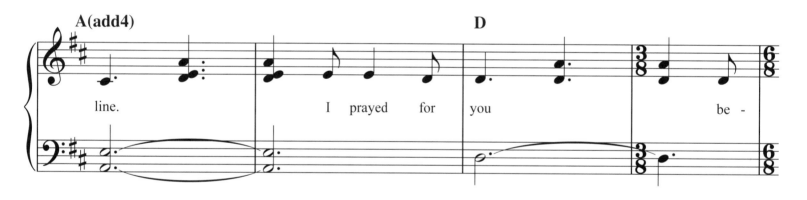

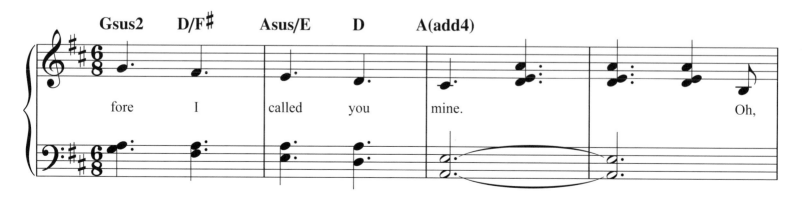

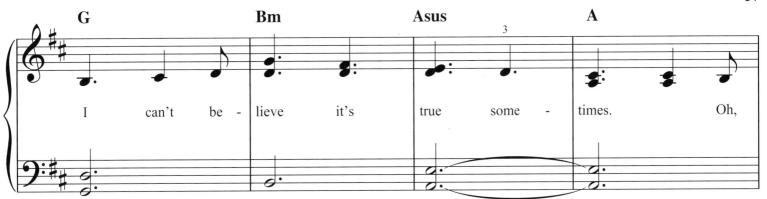

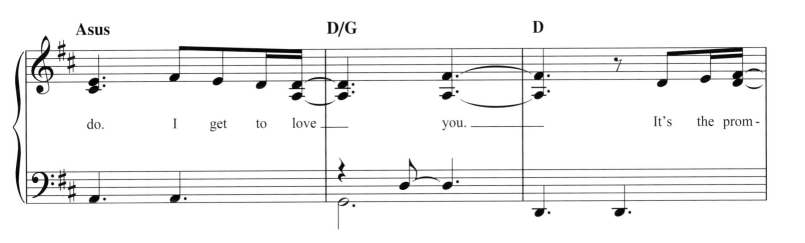

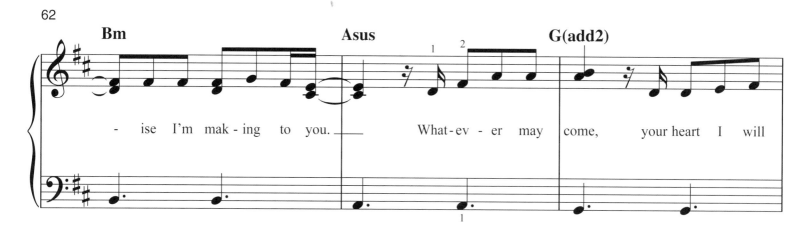

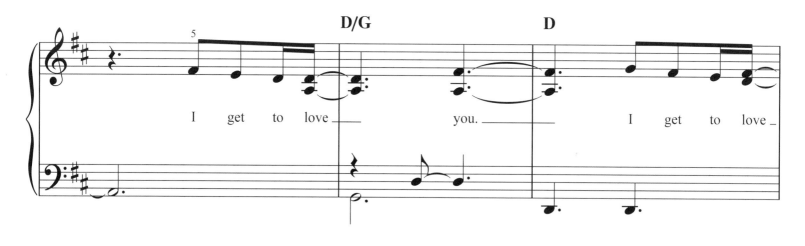

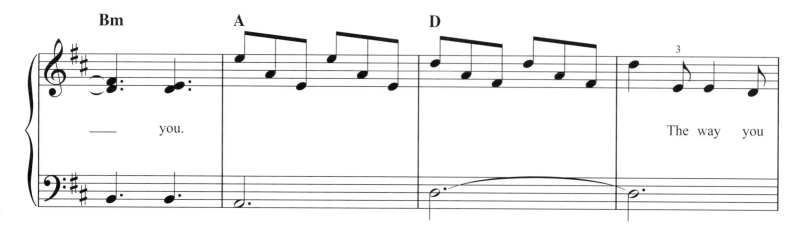

63

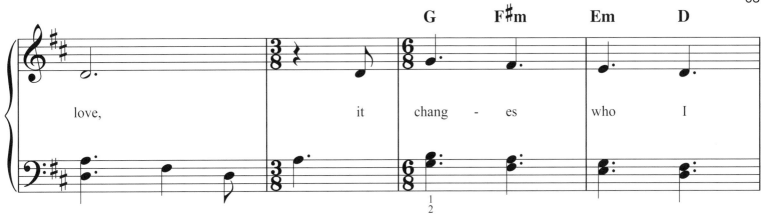

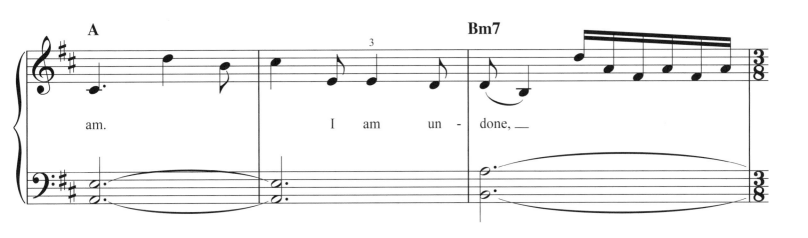

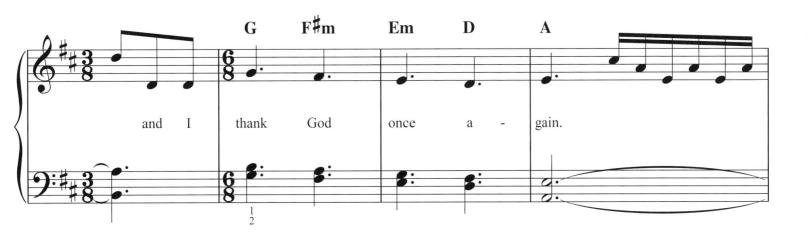

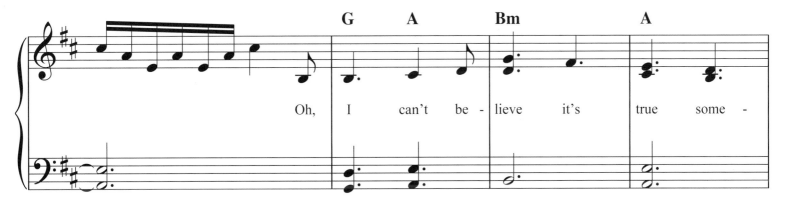

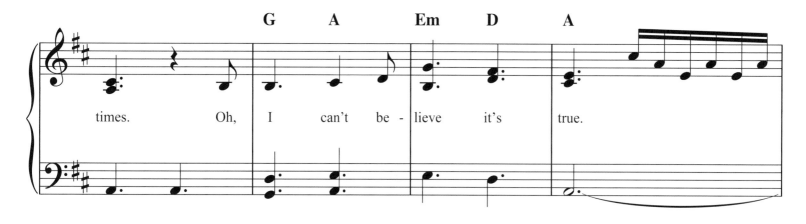

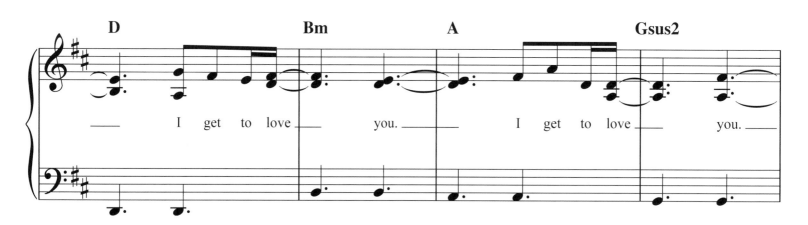

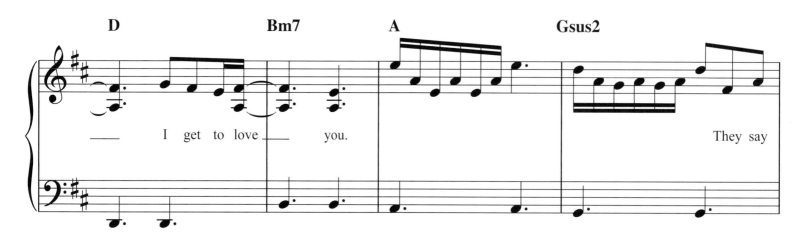

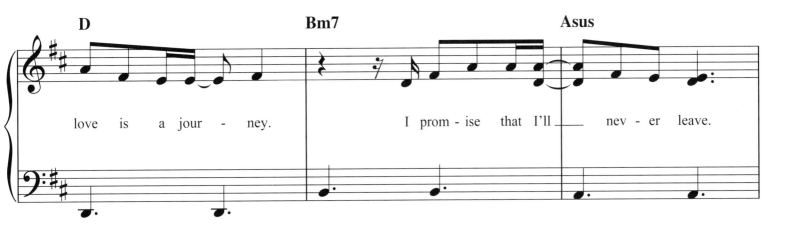

love is a jour - ney. I prom - ise that I'll ____ nev - er leave.

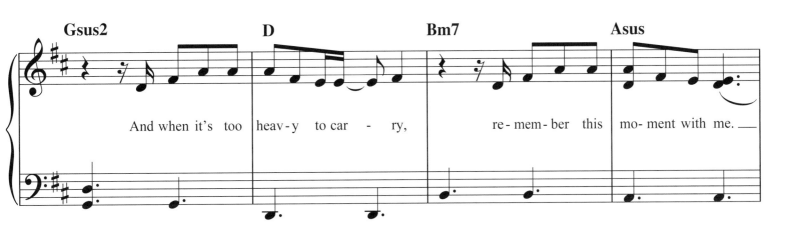

And when it's too heav-y to car - ry, re-mem-ber this mo-ment with me. ____

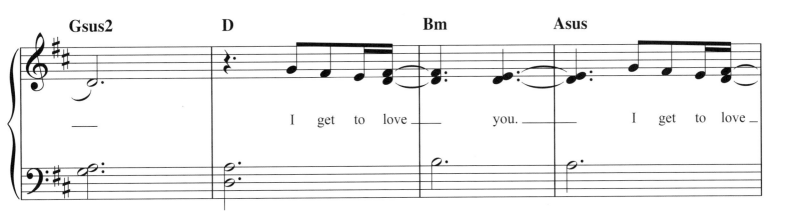

I get to love ____ you. ____ I get to love ____

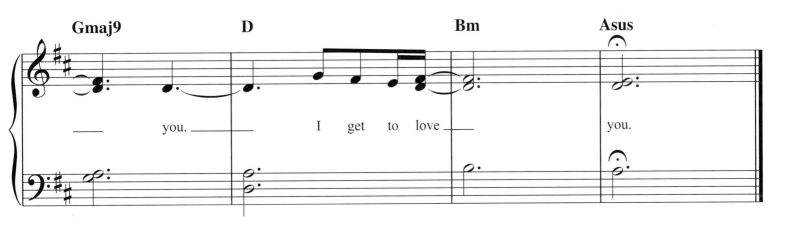

____ you. ____ I get to love ____ you.

I JUST CAN'T STOP LOVING YOU

Words and Music by
MICHAEL JACKSON

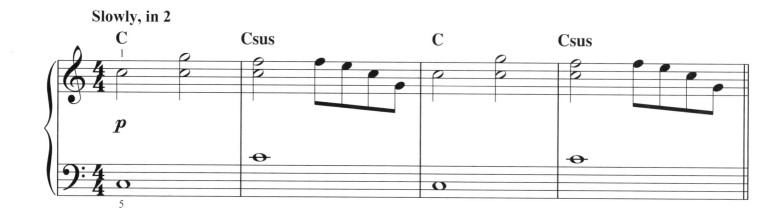

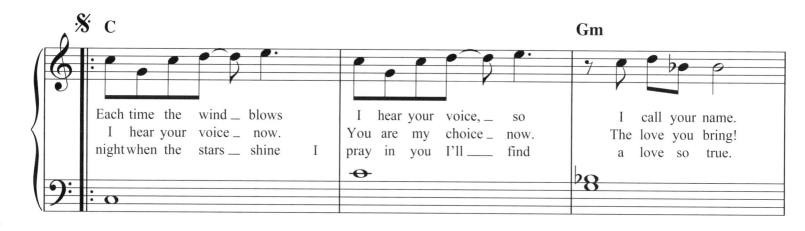

Each time the wind ___ blows
I hear your voice ___ now.
night when the stars ___ shine I

I hear your voice, ___ so
You are my choice ___ now.
pray in you I'll ___ find

I call your name.
The love you bring!
a love so true.

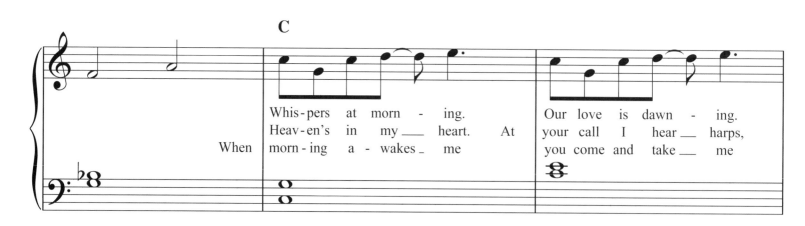

Whis-pers at morn - ing.
Heav-en's in my ___ heart. At
When morn-ing a - wakes ___ me

Our love is dawn - ing.
your call I hear ___ harps,
you come and take ___ me

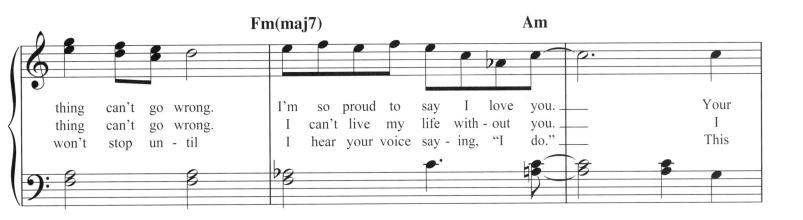

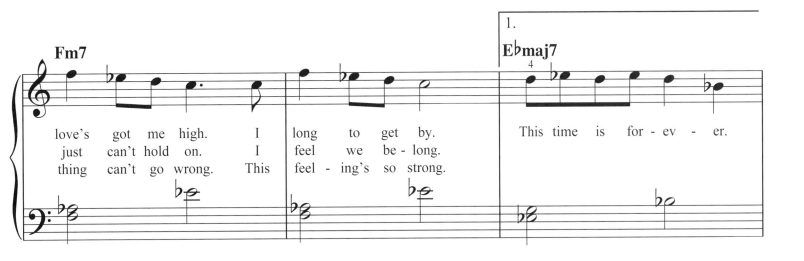

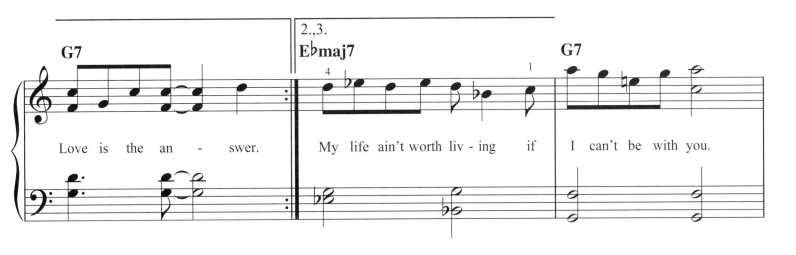

I just can't stop lov-ing you.

I just can't stop lov-ing you.

And if I stop, then tell me, just what will I

do? 'Cause I just can't stop lov-ing you.

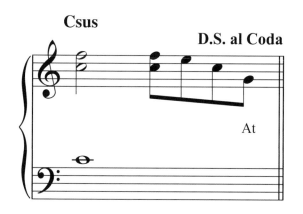

At

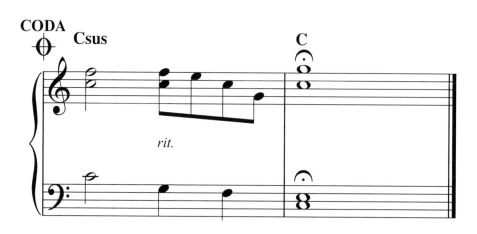

rit.

I'LL BE THERE

Words and Music by BERRY GORDY JR.,
HAL DAVIS, WILLIE HUTCH
and BOB WEST

Moderately

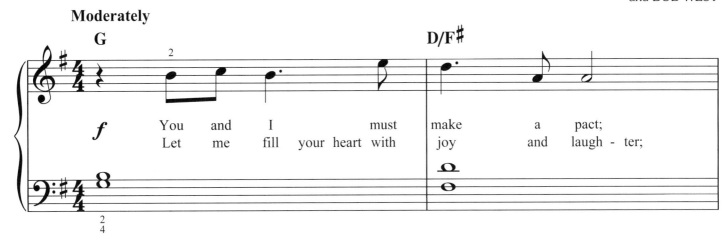

You and I must make a pact;
Let me fill your heart with joy and laugh-ter;

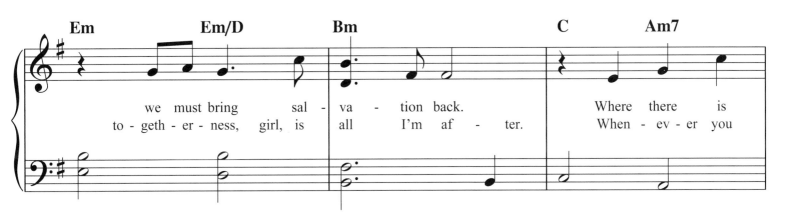

we must bring sal - va - tion back. Where there is
to - geth - er - ness, girl, is all I'm af - ter. When - ev - er you

love, I'll be there.
need me, I'll be there.

I'll reach out my hand to you; I'll have faith in
I'll be there to pro - tect you with un - self - ish love that

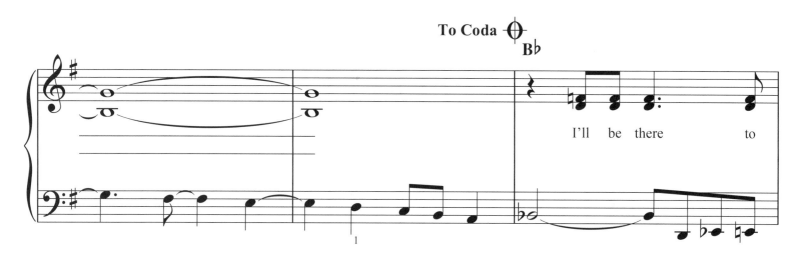

I ONLY HAVE EYES FOR YOU

from DAMES

Words by AL DUBIN
Music by HARRY WARREN

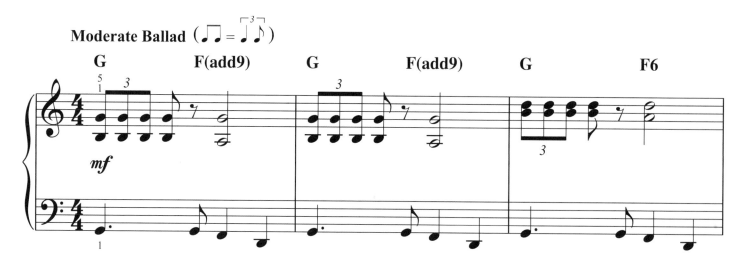

Are the stars out to-night? I don't

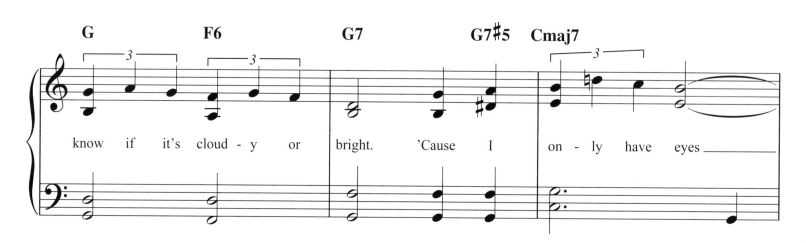

know if it's cloud-y or bright. 'Cause I on-ly have eyes _____

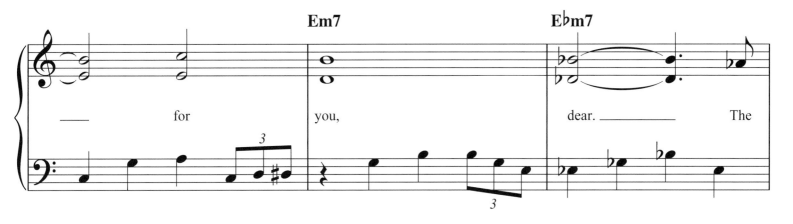

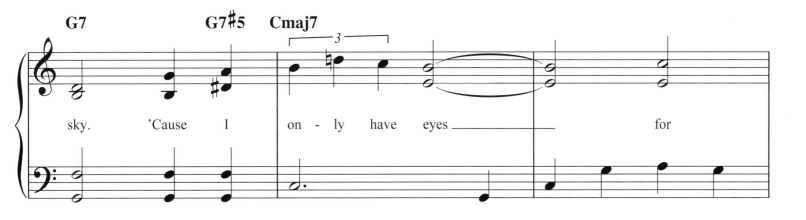

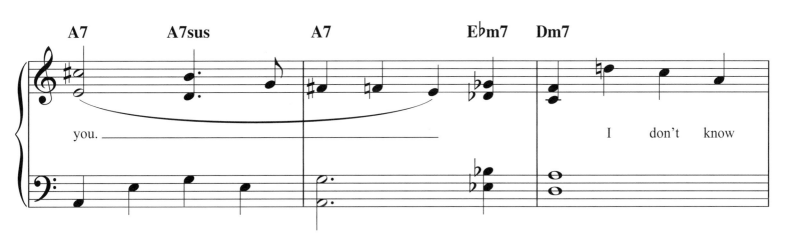

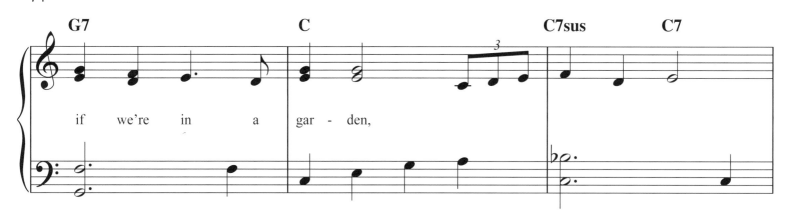

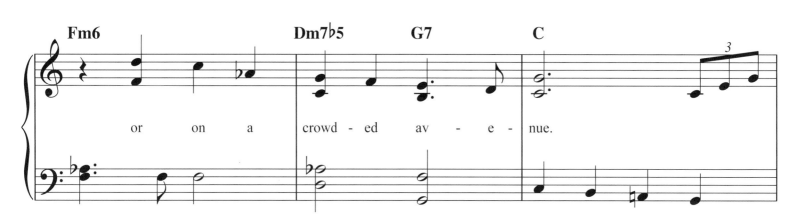

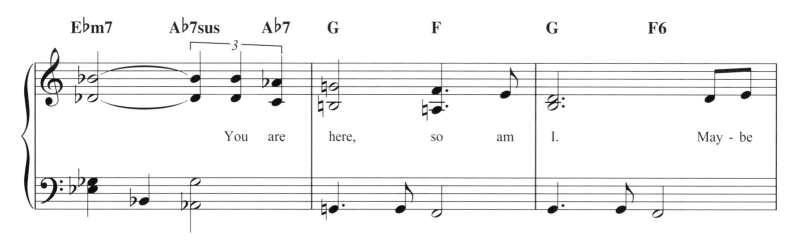

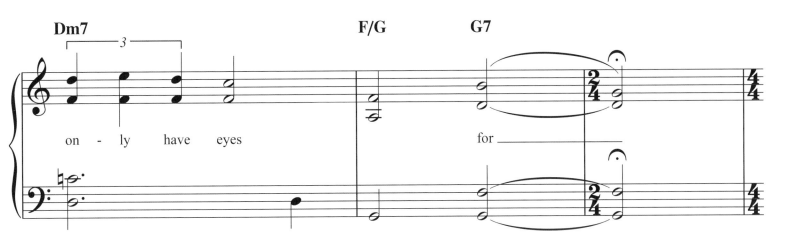

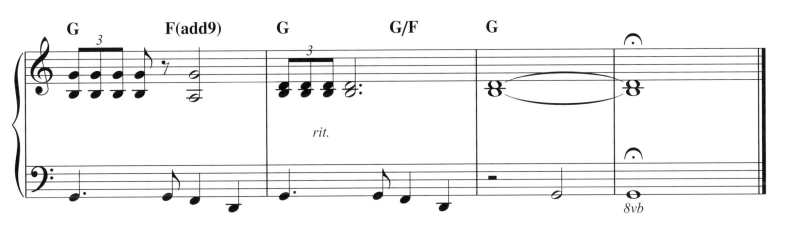

I SAY A LITTLE PRAYER

Lyric by HAL DAVID
Music by BURT BACHARACH

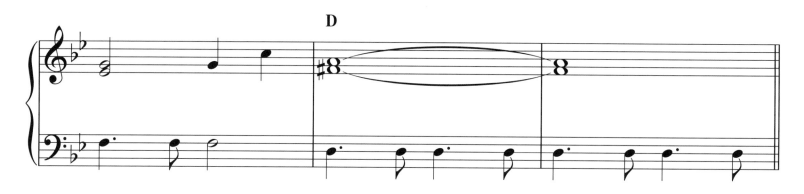

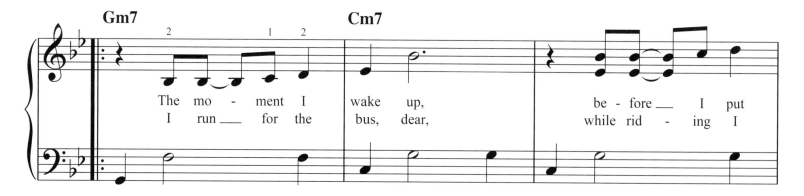

The mo - ment I wake up, be - fore ___ I put
I run ___ for the bus, dear, while rid - ing I

on my make - up, ___ I say a lit - tle prayer for
think of us, dear. ___ I say a lit - tle prayer for

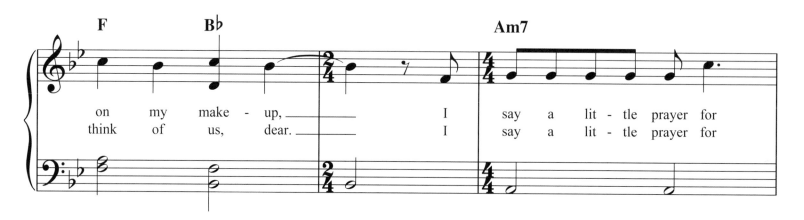

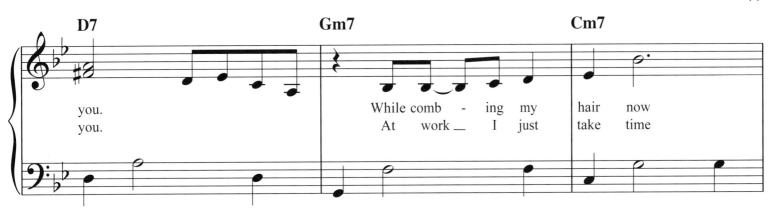

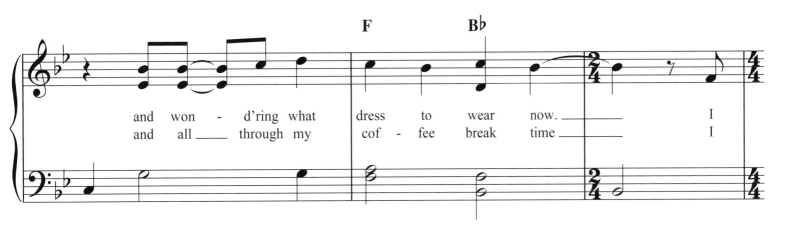

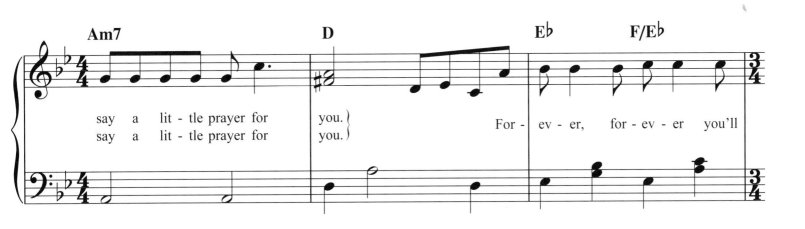

77

78

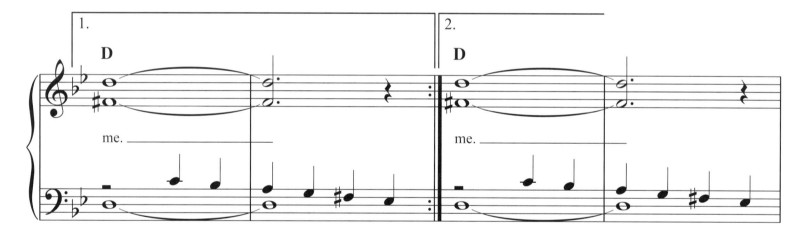

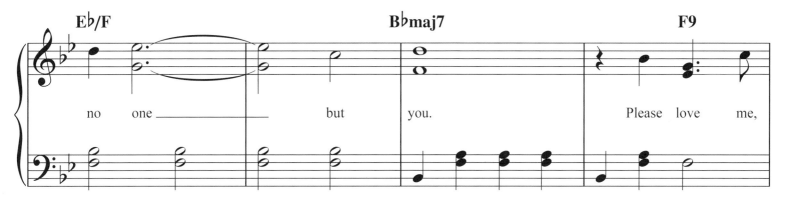

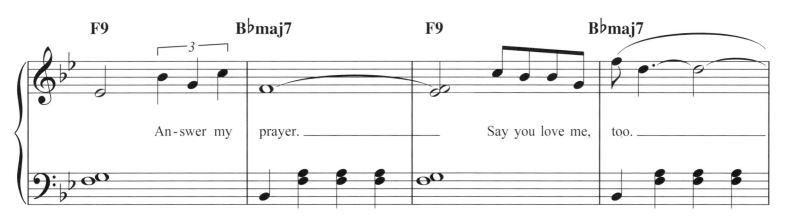

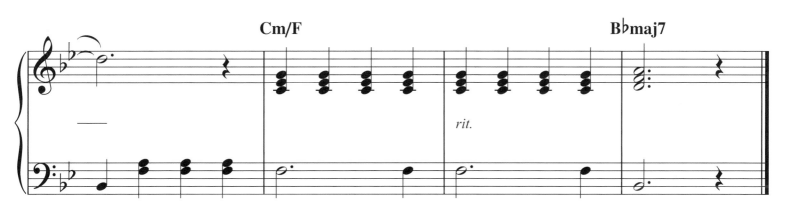

I WILL ALWAYS LOVE YOU

Words and Music by
DOLLY PARTON

If
sweet

should stay,
mem - o - ries,

I would
that's all

on - ly be in your
I am tak - ing with

way.
me.

So I'll go,
Good - bye,

but I
please don't

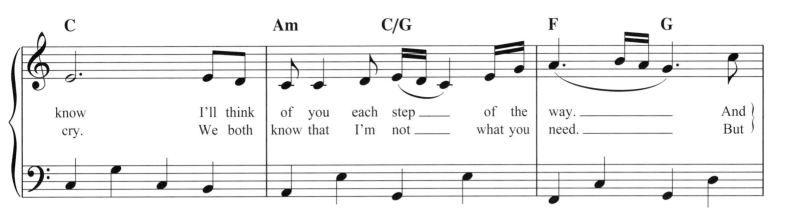

know   I'll think   of   you   each   step ____   of   the   way. _____   And
cry.   We   both   know   that   I'm   not ____   what   you   need. _____   But

I _____   will   al   -   ways __   love _   you. _____   I ____   will

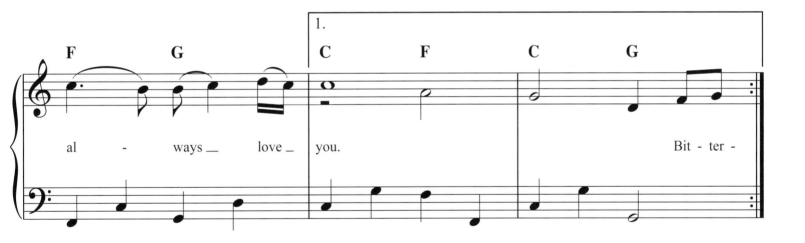

al   -   ways __   love _   you.   Bit - ter -

you. _____   I   will   al-ways   love   you.

I'LL HAVE TO SAY I LOVE YOU IN A SONG

Words and Music by
JIM CROCE

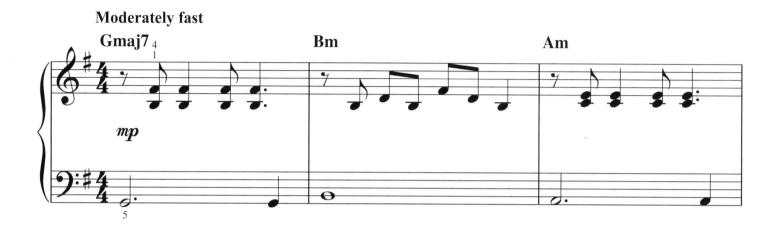

Well, I | know it's kind of late. ____
know it's kind of strange, _

I hope I did-n't | wake you, but what I
but ev-'ry time I'm | near you, I just

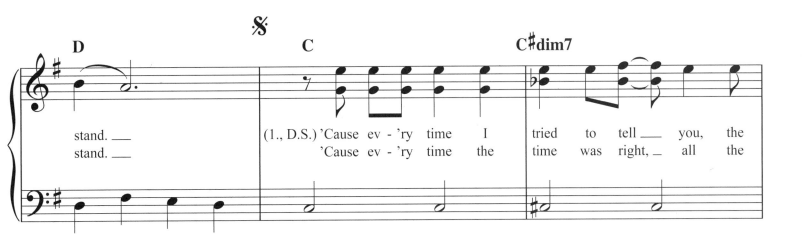

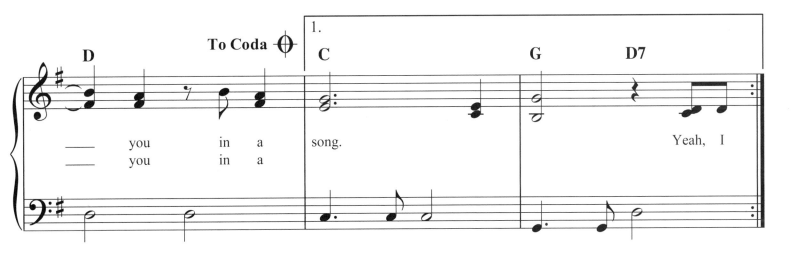

song.   Yeah, I   know   it's   kind   of   late.__

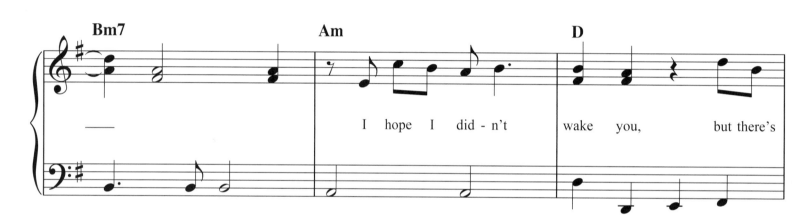

—   I   hope   I   did - n't   wake   you,   but there's

some-thin' that I just got to say. __   I know you'd un - der -

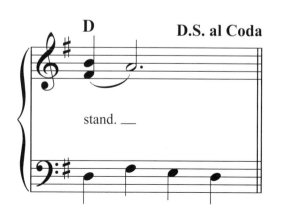

stand. __

song.   *rit.*

I'LL STAND BY YOU

Words and Music by CHRISSIE HYNDE,
TOM KELLY and BILLY STEINBERG

When the night falls on you, you don't know what to do. Noth-ing you con-

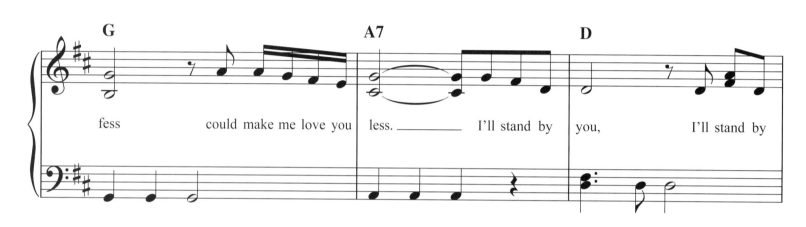

fess   could make me love you   less. _____ I'll stand by   you,   I'll stand by

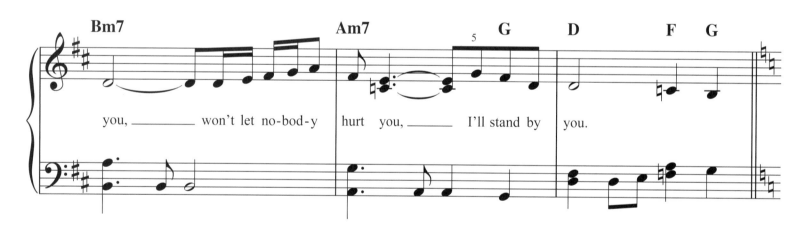

you, _____ won't let no-bod-y hurt you, _____ I'll stand by   you.

So,   if you're mad, get   mad; _____ don't hold it all in-

87

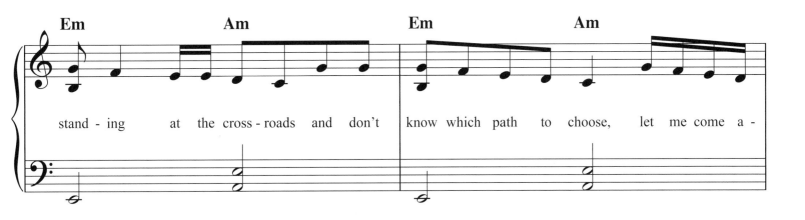

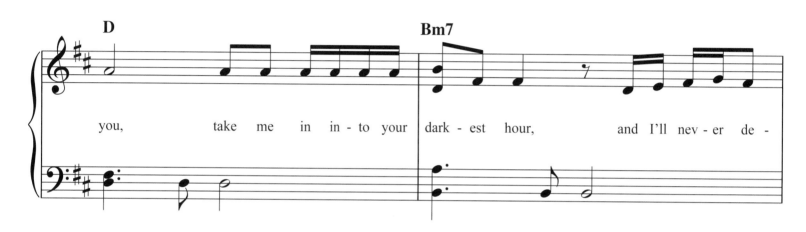

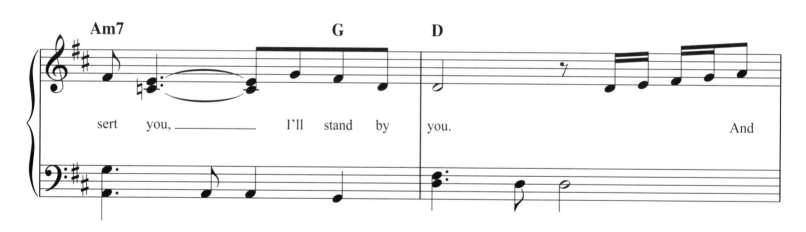

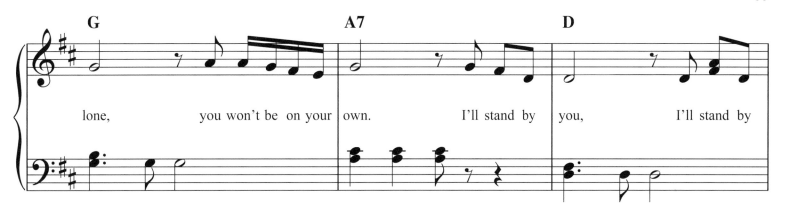

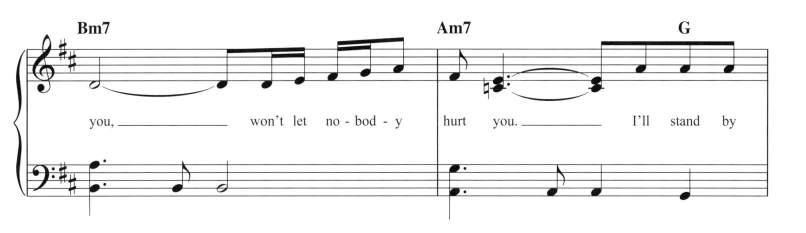

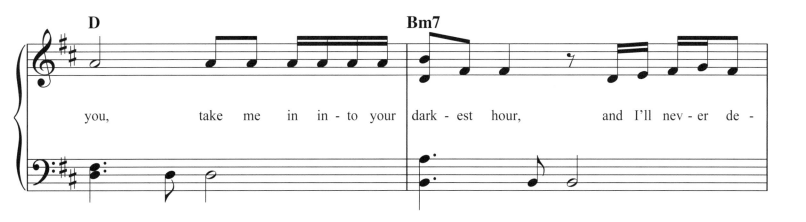

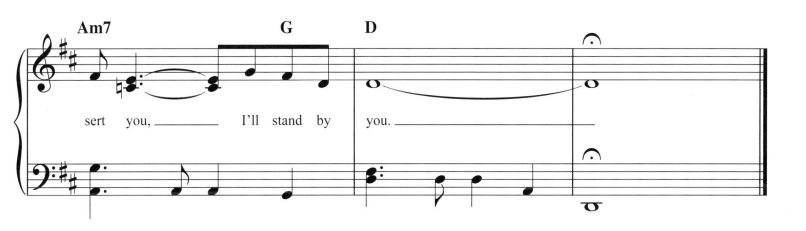

I'LL NEVER LOVE THIS WAY AGAIN

Words and Music by RICHARD KERR
and WILL JENNINGS

Slow Ballad

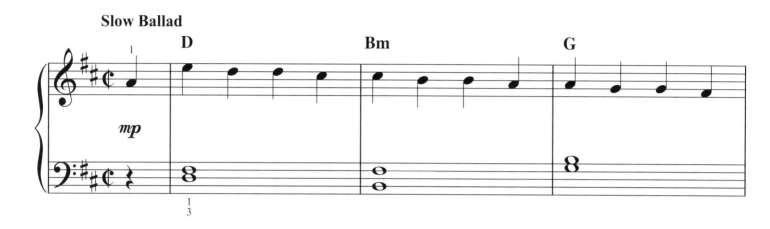

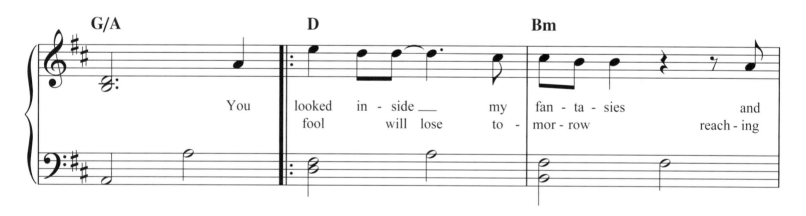

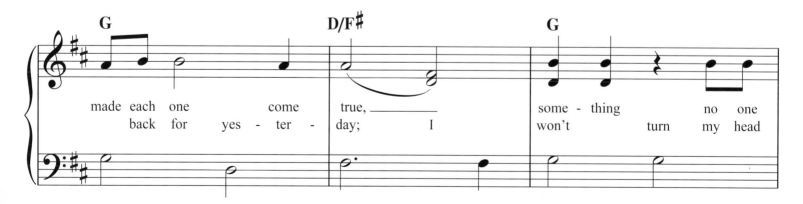

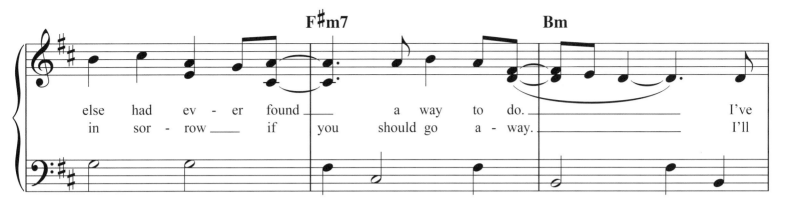

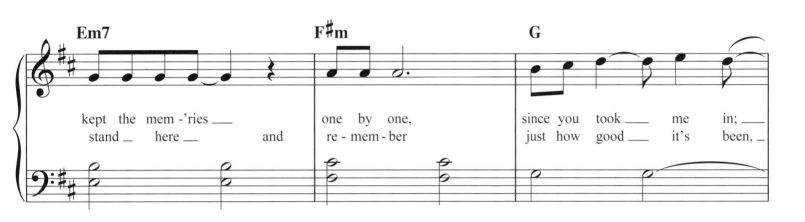

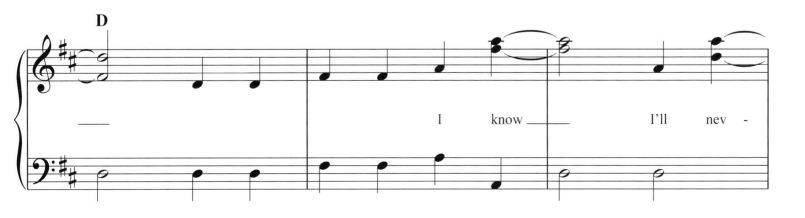

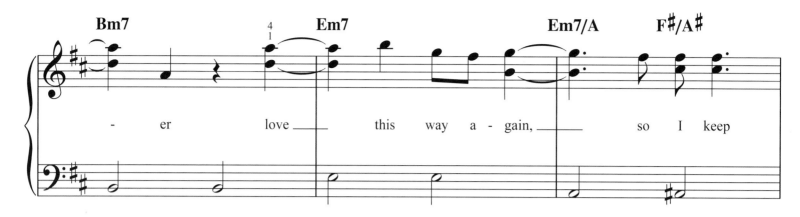

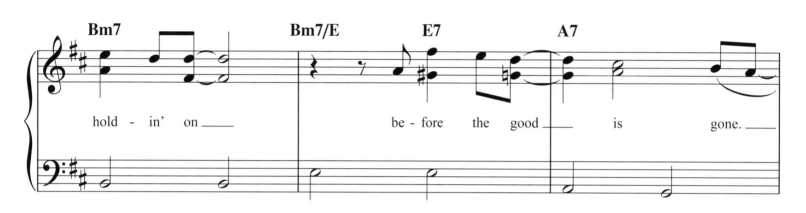

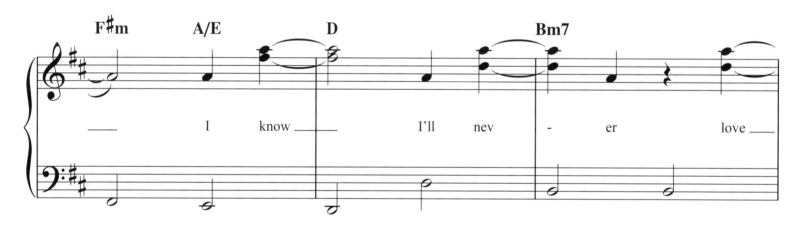

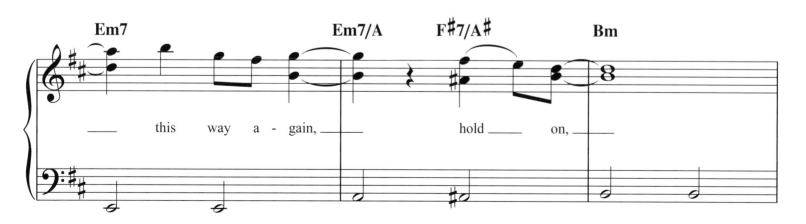

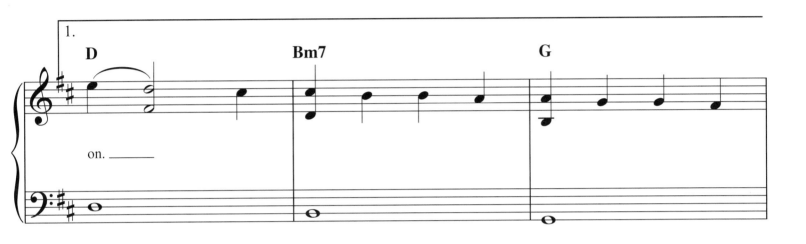

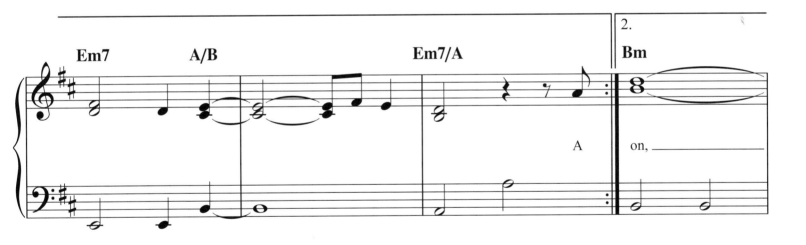

I'M YOURS

Words and Music by
JASON MRAZ

1. Well,
2. (See additional lyrics)

you done done me in; you bet I felt it. I tried to be chill, but you're so hot that I melt-ed. I

fell right through the cracks. _ Now I'm try-ing to get back. _____ Be-fore the

cool done run out, I'll be giv-ing it my best- est, and noth-ing's gon-na stop me but di-vine in-ter-ven-tion. I

reck-on it's a-gain my turn to win some or learn some. But I ___ won't hes-i-

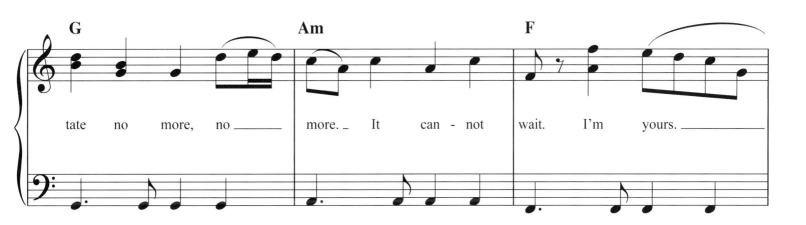

tate no more, no _____ more. _ It can-not wait. I'm yours. _____

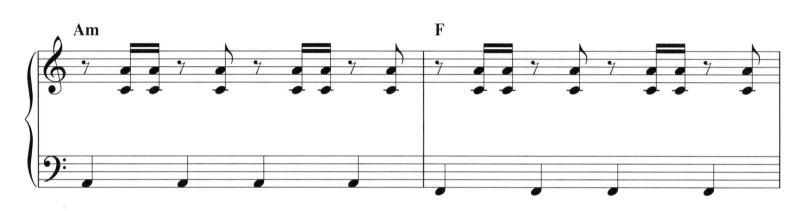

Well, o - pen up your mind and see like me. O - pen up your plans and, damn, you're

free. Look in - to your heart __ and you'll find love, love, _____ love.

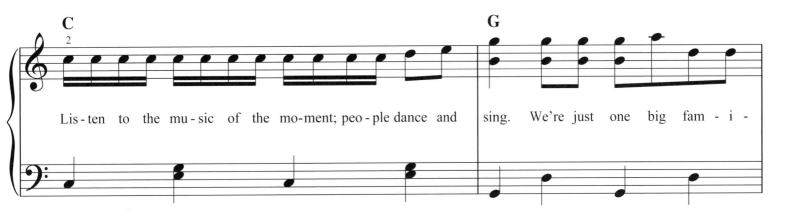

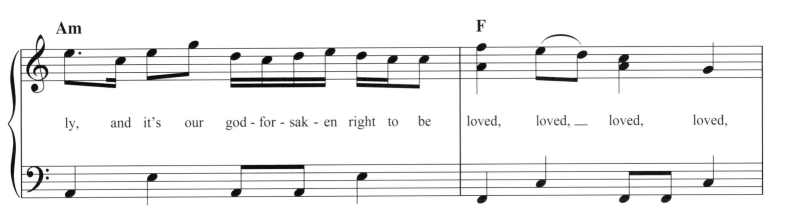

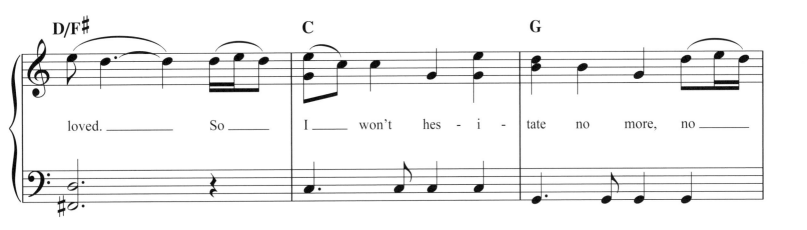

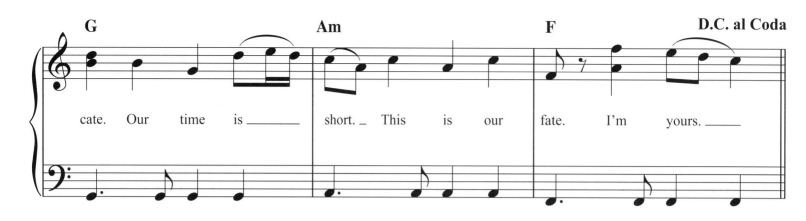

Additional Lyrics

2. I've been spending way too long
Checking my tongue in the mirror
And bending over backwards
Just to try to see it clearer.
But my breath fogged up the glass,
And so I drew a new face and I laughed.
I guess what I'll be saying
Is there ain't no better reason
To rid yourself of vanities
And just go with the seasons.
It's what we aim to do.
Our name is our virtue.

But I won't hesitate no more...

IT HAD TO BE YOU

Words by GUS KAHN
Music by ISHAM JONES

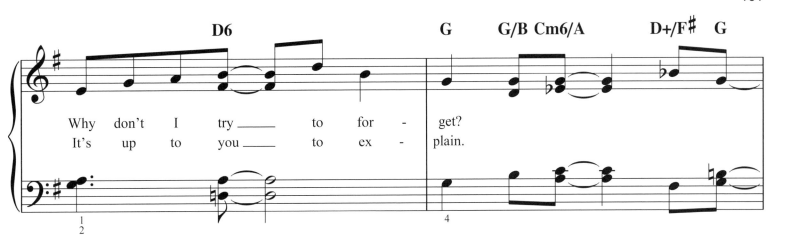

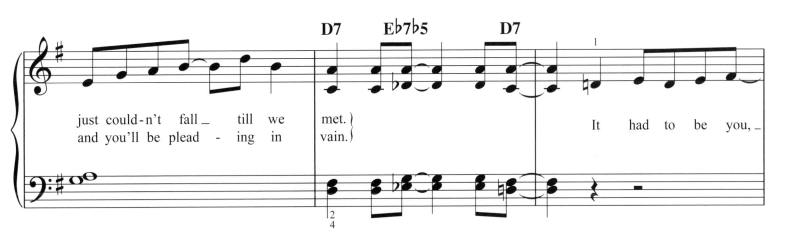

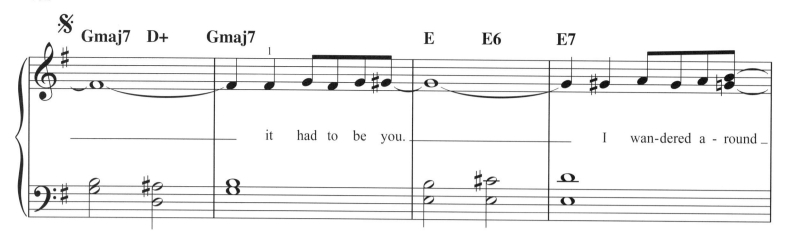

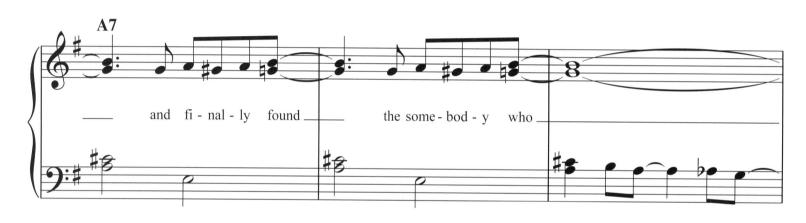

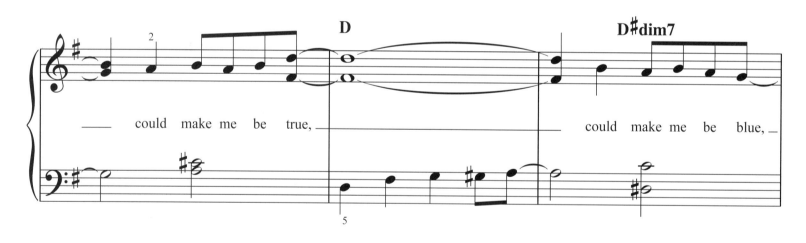

think-ing of you. Some oth-ers I've seen

might nev-er be mean,

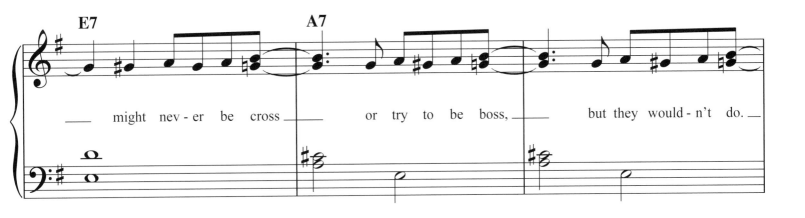

might nev-er be cross or try to be boss, but they would-n't do.

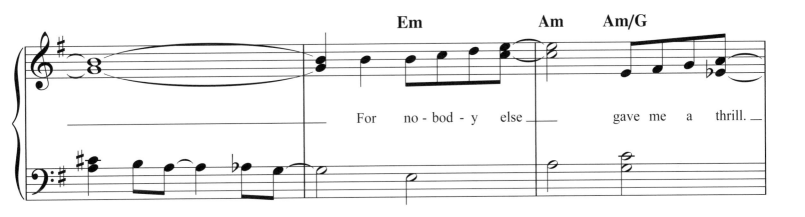

For no-bod-y else gave me a thrill.

With all your faults, I love you still. It had to be you,

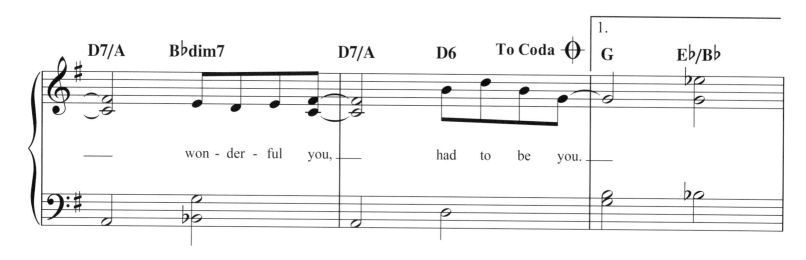

won - der - ful you, had to be you.

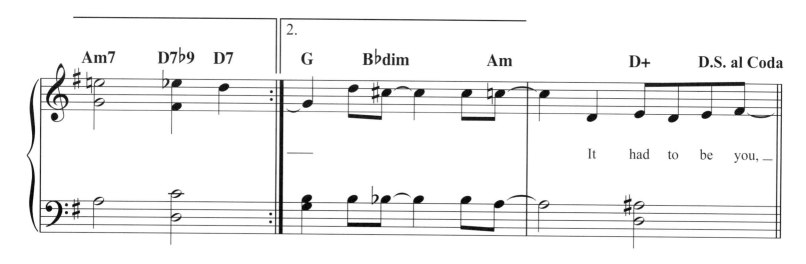

It had to be you,

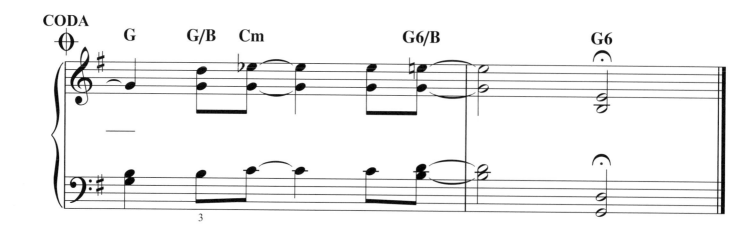

3

LOVE ME LIKE YOU DO

from FIFTY SHADES OF GREY

Words and Music by MAX MARTIN,
SAVAN KOTECHA, ILYA, ALI PAYAMI
and TOVE LO

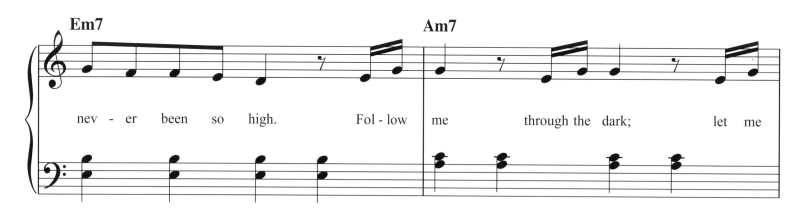

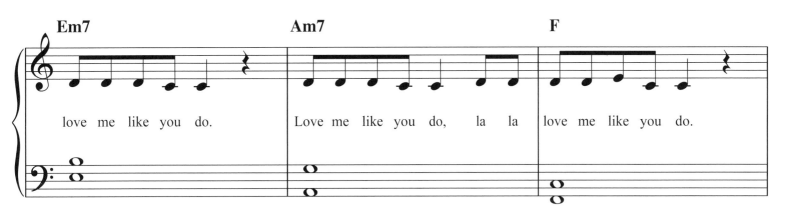

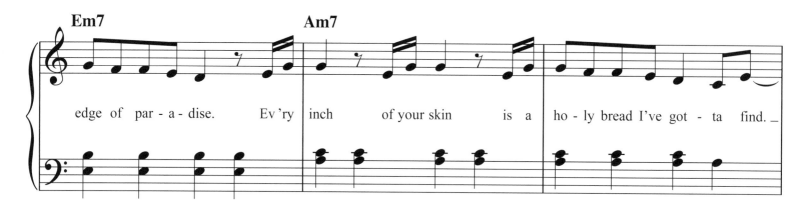

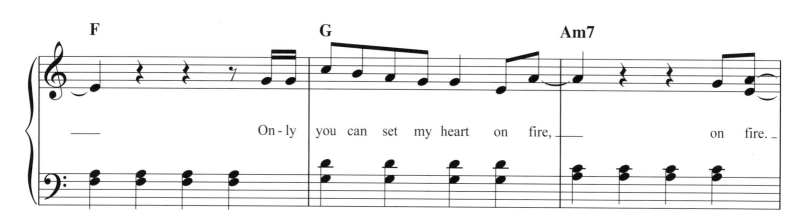

What are you wait - ing for? _____

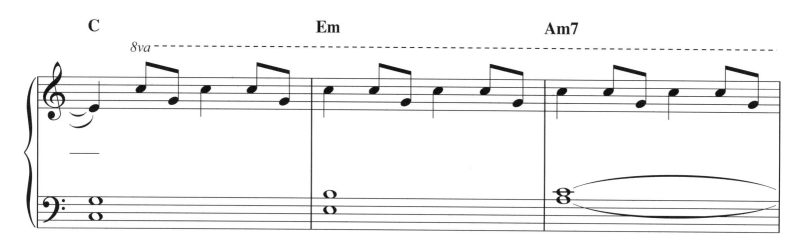

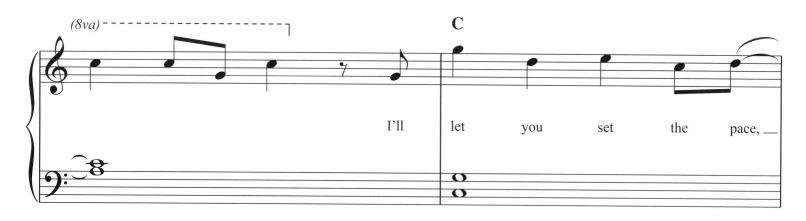

I'll let you set the pace, ___

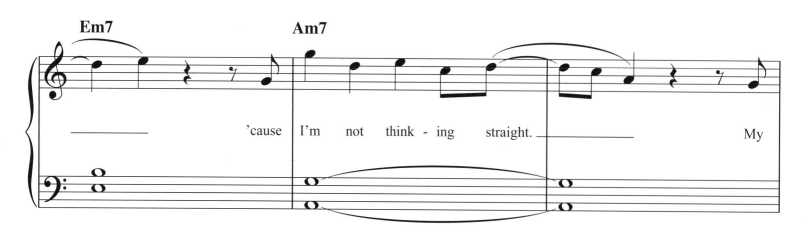

_____ 'cause I'm not think - ing straight. _____ My

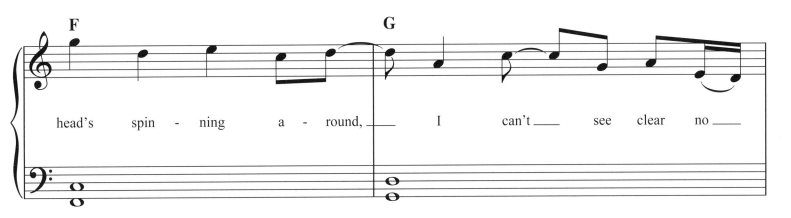

head's spin - ning a - round, ____ I can't ____ see clear no ____

more. What are you wait - ing for?

CODA

What are you wait - ing for? ____

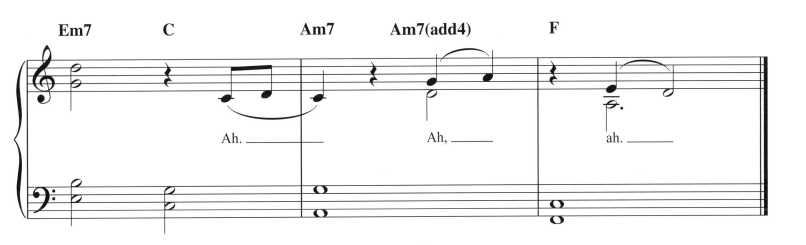

Ah. ____ Ah, ____ ah. ____

JUST GIVE ME A REASON

Words and Music by ALECIA MOORE,
JEFF BHASKER and NATE RUESS

F   C   Am   D/F♯

ev - 'ry touch, you fixed them.   Now   you've been talk - ing in your
it's   all in your mind.   You've been hav - ing real bad

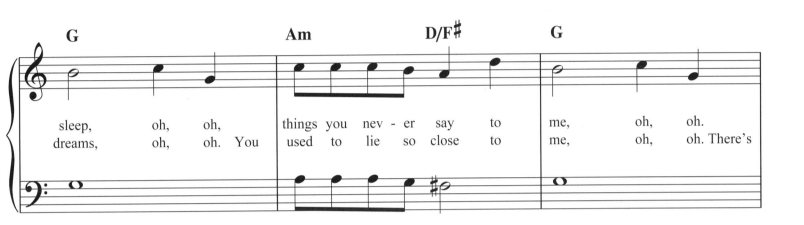

G   Am   D/F♯   G

sleep,   oh,   oh,   things you nev - er say to   me,   oh,   oh.
dreams,   oh,   oh. You   used to lie so close to   me,   oh,   oh. There's

To Coda ⊕

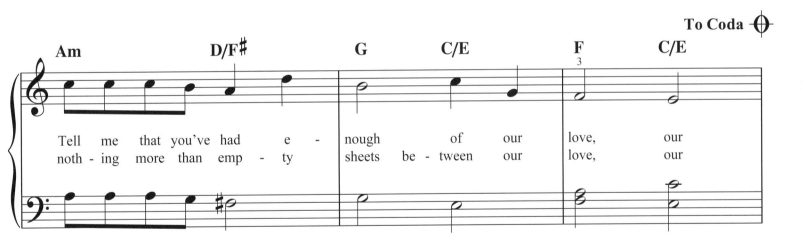

Am   D/F♯   G   C/E   F   C/E

Tell me that you've had e - nough of our   love,   our
noth - ing more than emp - ty sheets be - tween our   love,   our

Gsus   G   C   G/B

love.   Just give me a rea - son, just a   lit - tle bit's e - nough, just a

mf

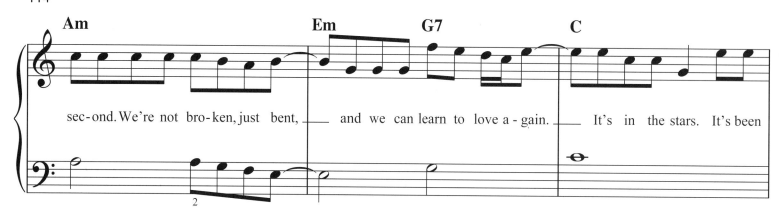

sec-ond. We're not bro-ken, just bent, and we can learn to love a-gain. It's in the stars. It's been

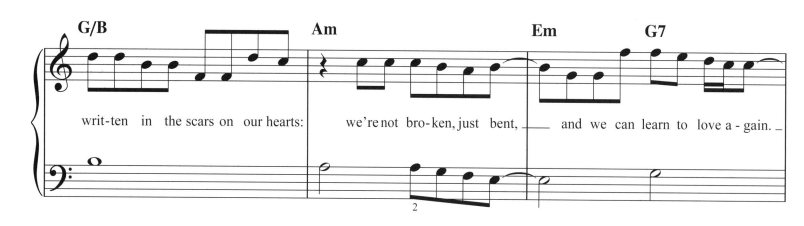

writ-ten in the scars on our hearts: we're not bro-ken, just bent, and we can learn to love a-gain.

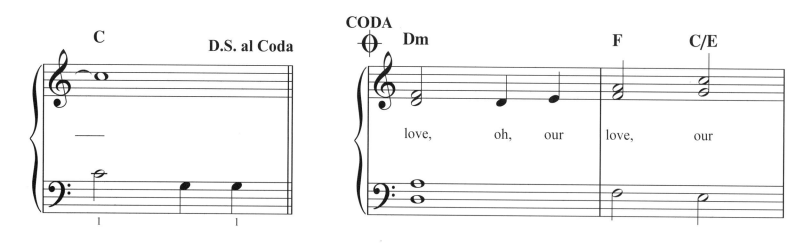

love, oh, our love, our

love. Just give me a rea-son, just a lit-tle bit's e-nough, just a

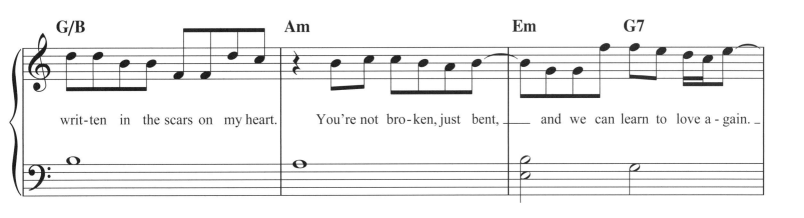

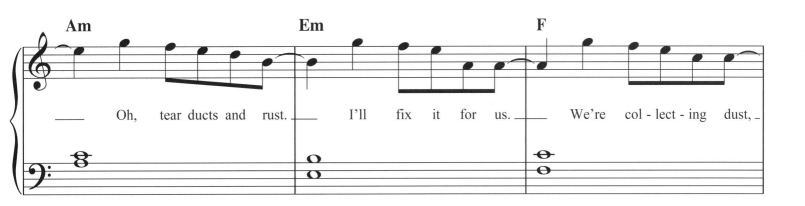

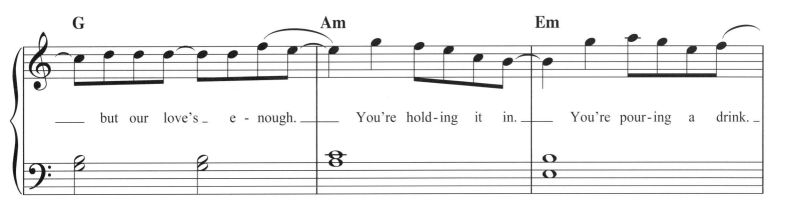

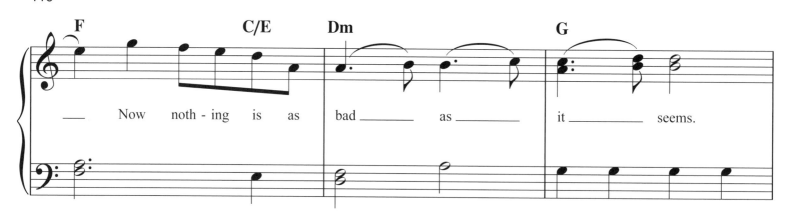

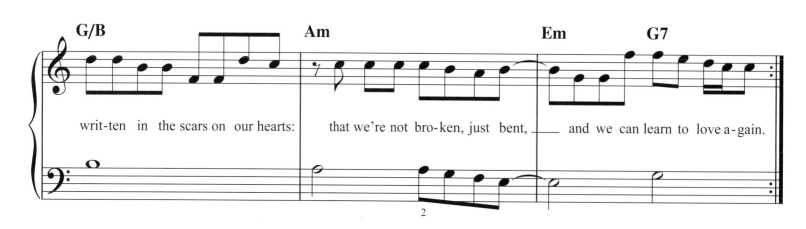

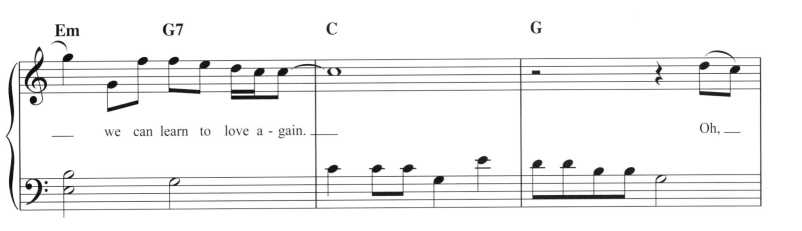

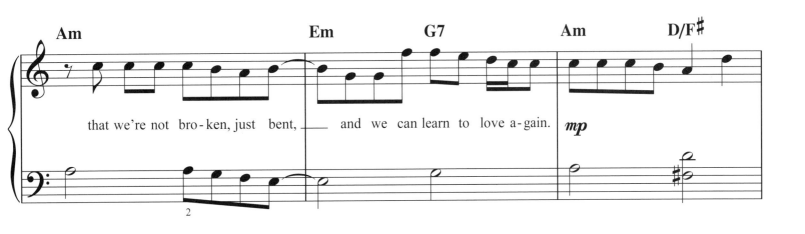

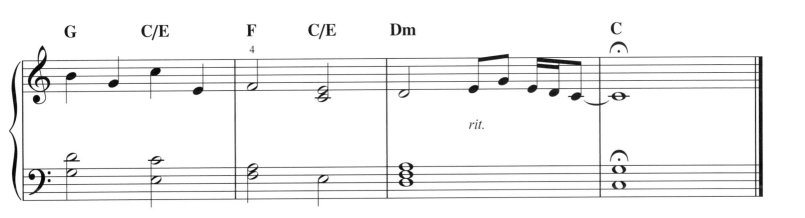

MY GIRL

Words and Music by SMOKEY ROBINSON
and RONALD WHITE

119

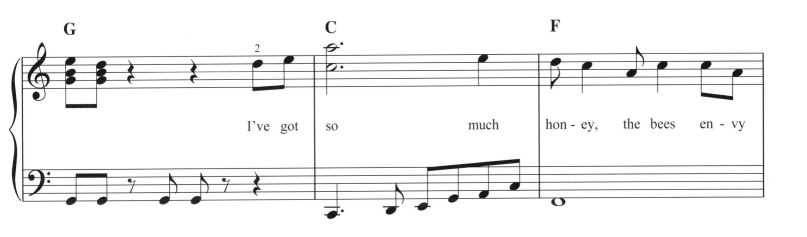

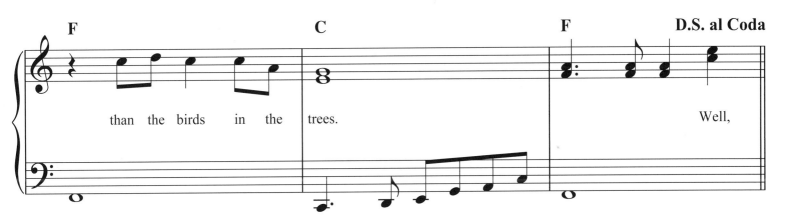

CODA

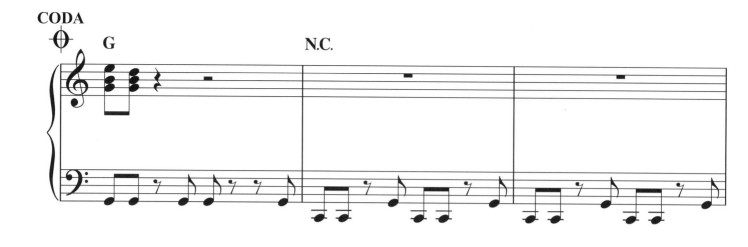

I don't need no mon - ey,

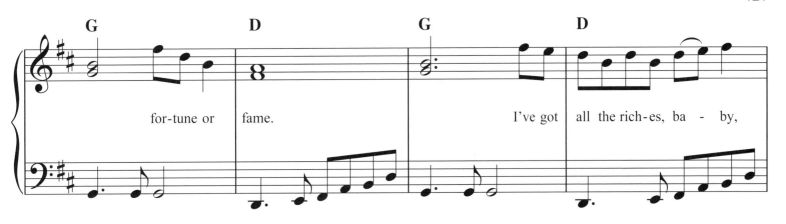

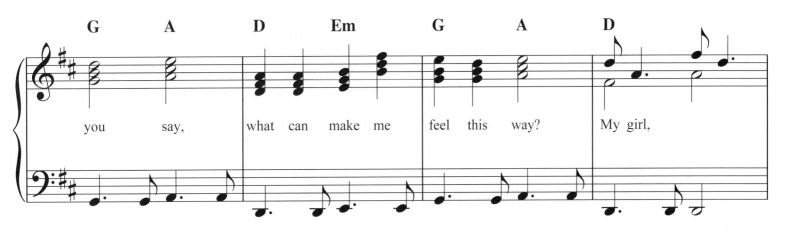

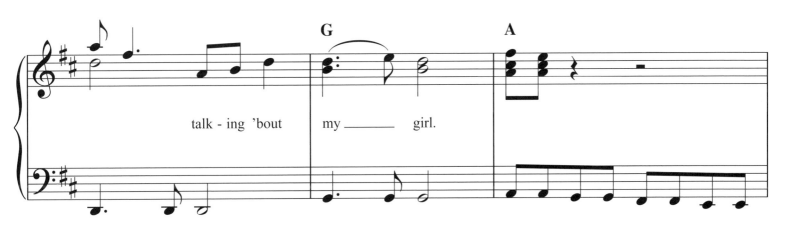

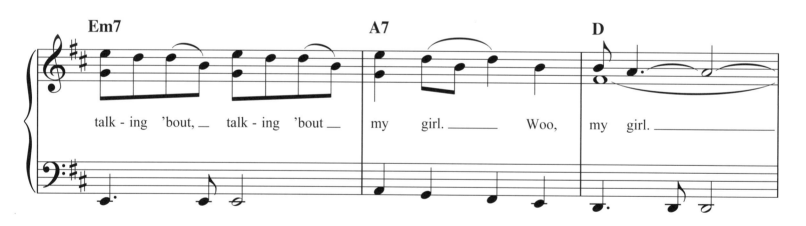

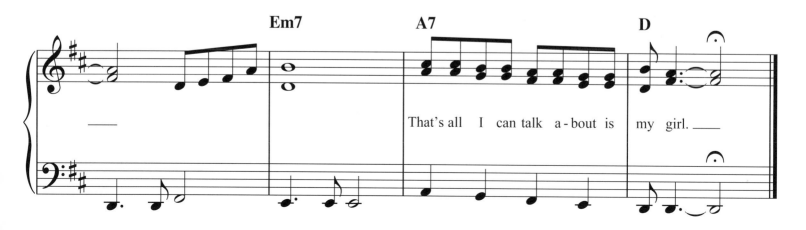

SIGNED, SEALED, DELIVERED I'M YOURS

Words and Music by STEVIE WONDER,
SYREETA WRIGHT, LEE GARRETT
and LULA MAE HARDAWAY

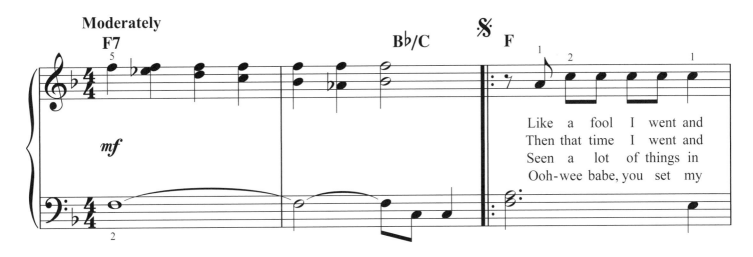

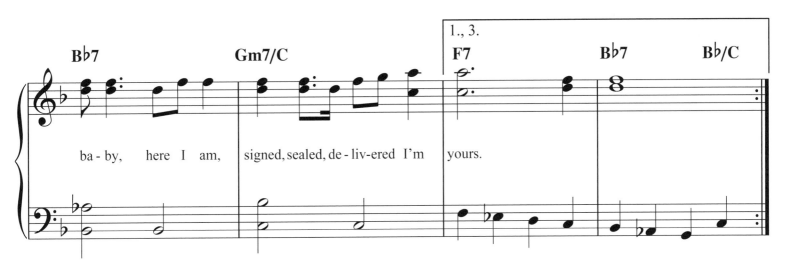

124

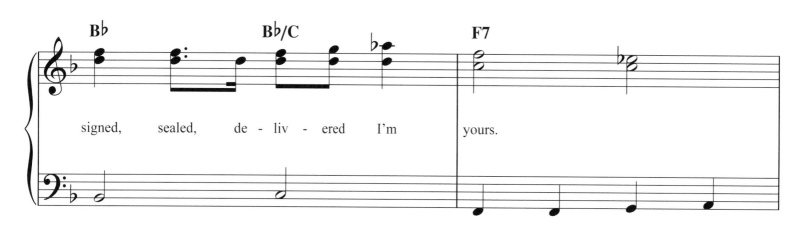

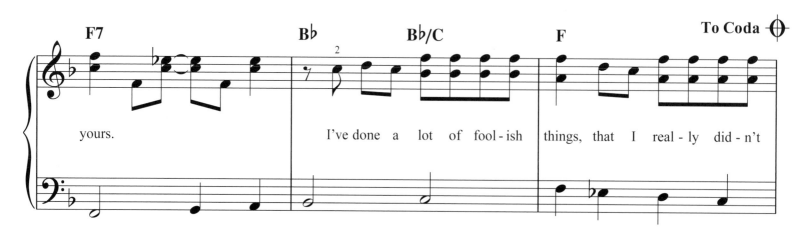

D.S. al Coda
(with repeat)

mean. Hey, — hey, yeah, yeah, did -n't I, oh ba - by.

mean. I could be a bro-ken man, but here I am with your fu - ture, got your fu -

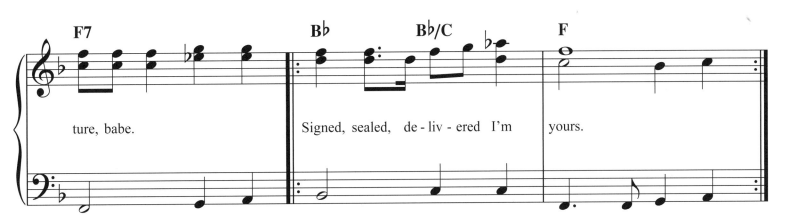

ture, babe. Signed, sealed, de - liv - ered I'm yours.

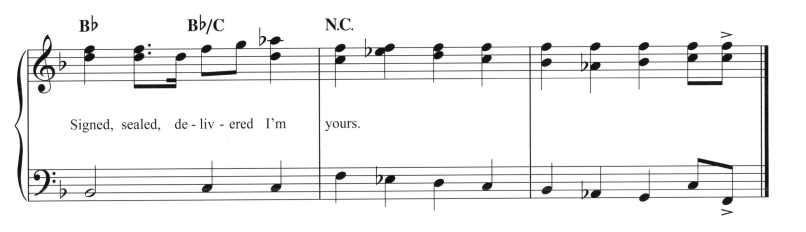

Signed, sealed, de - liv - ered I'm yours.

MY HEART WILL GO ON
(Love Theme from 'Titanic')
from the Paramount and Twentieth Century Fox Motion Picture TITANIC

Music by JAMES HORNER
Lyric by WILL JENNINGS

Moderately

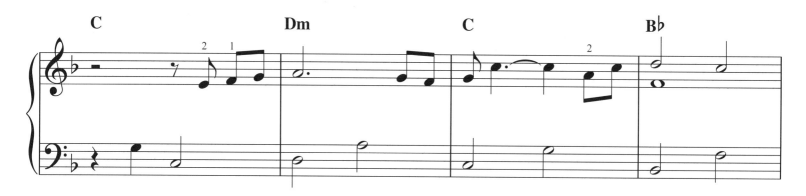

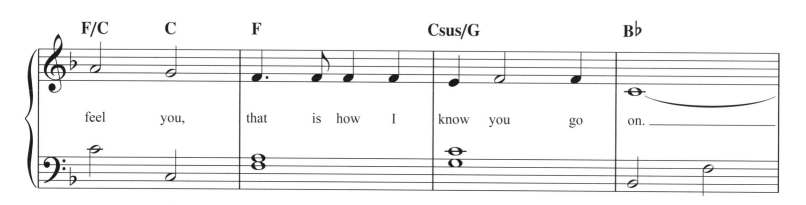

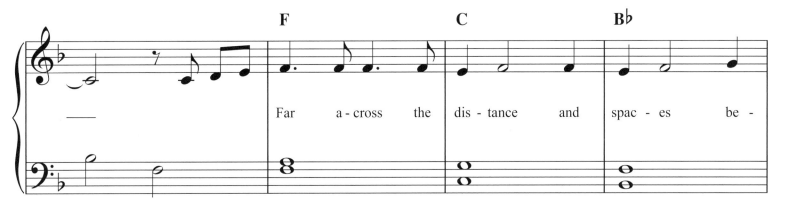

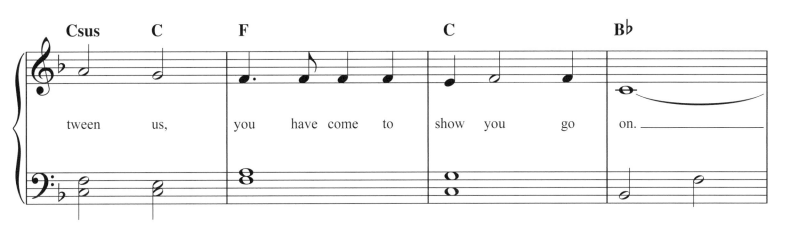

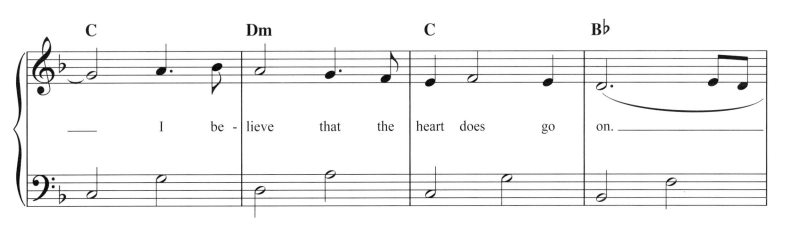

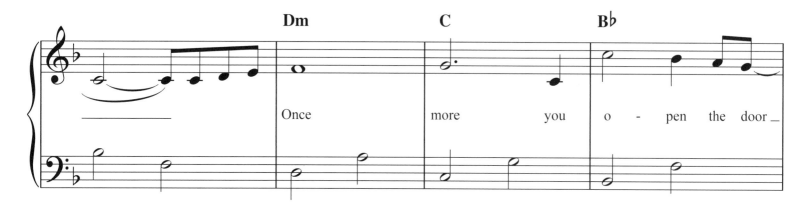

Once more you o - pen the door_

_ and you're here in my heart, and my heart will go

on and on.

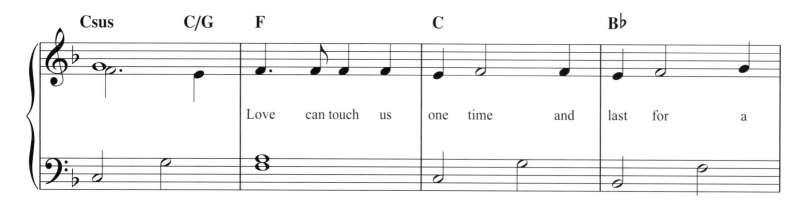

Love can touch us one time and last for a

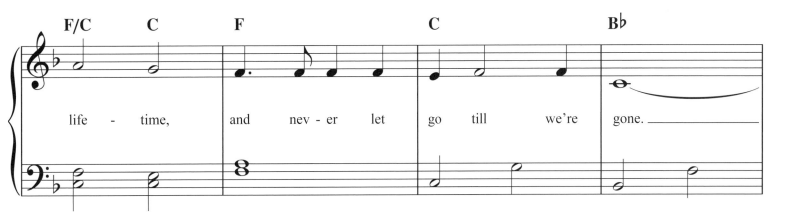

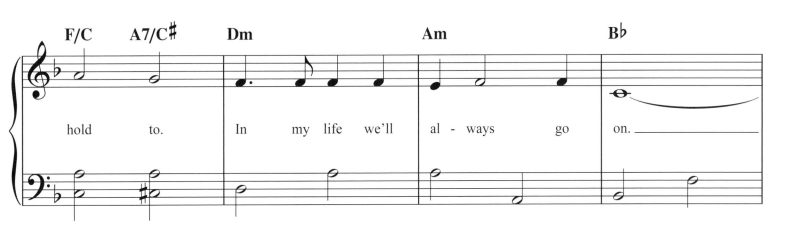

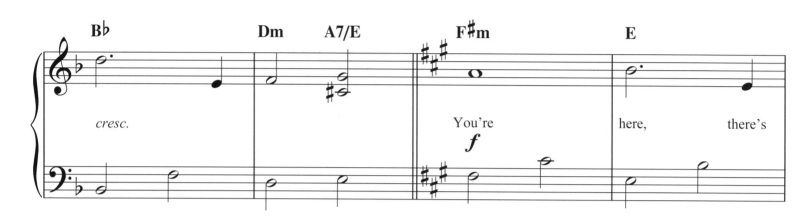

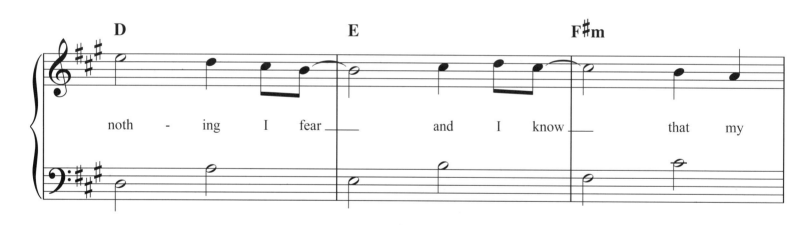

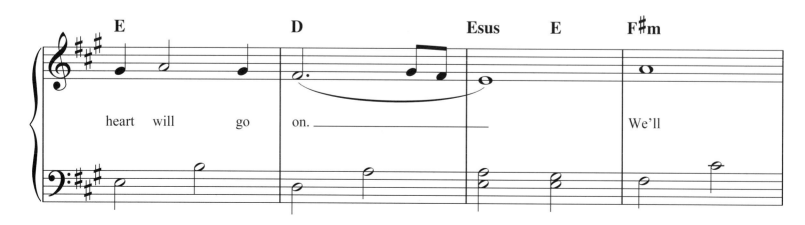

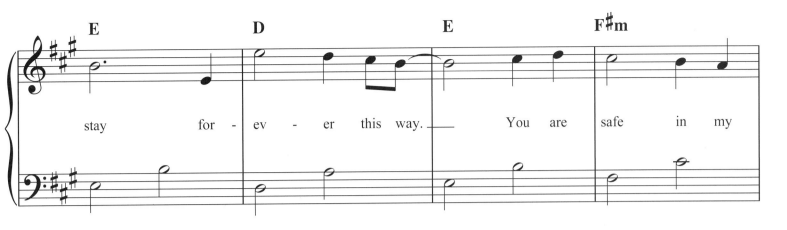

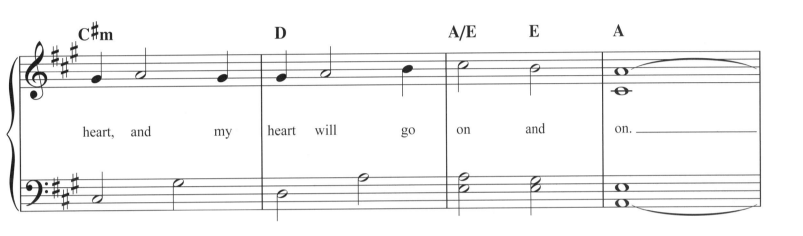

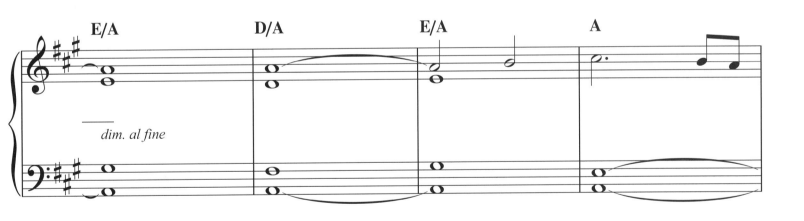

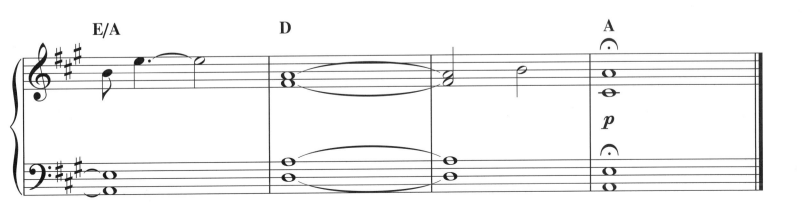

NEED YOU NOW

Words and Music by HILLARY SCOTT,
CHARLES KELLEY, DAVE HAYWOOD
and JOSH KEAR

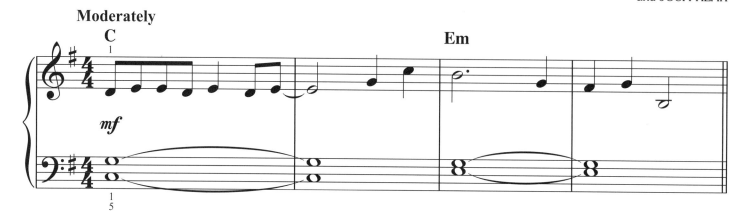

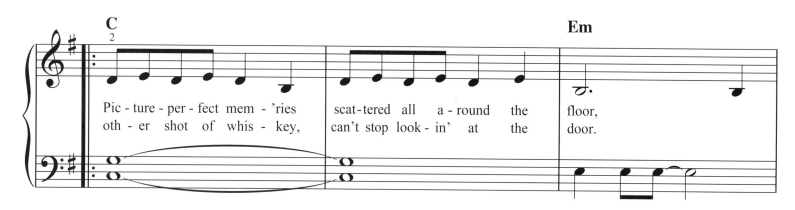

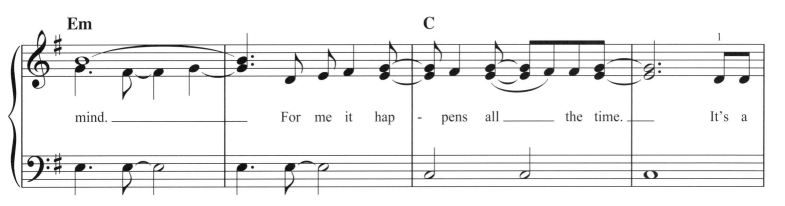

mind. _____ For me it hap - pens all _____ the time. ___ It's a

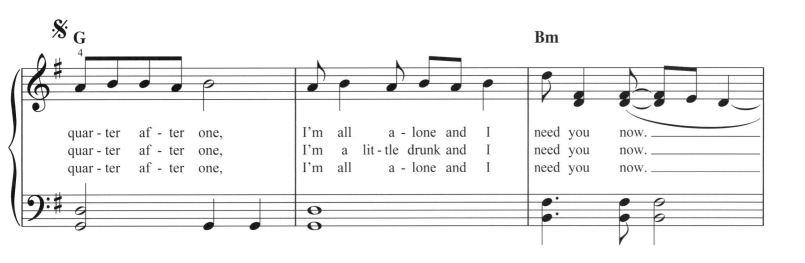

quar - ter af - ter one,   I'm all   a - lone and I   need you   now. _____
quar - ter af - ter one,   I'm a lit - tle drunk and I   need you   now. _____
quar - ter af - ter one,   I'm all   a - lone and I   need you   now. _____

_____ Said I would-n't call, but I   lost all   con - trol
_____ Said I would-n't call, but I   lost all   con - trol } and I
_____ Said I would-n't call, but __   I'm a lit - tle drunk }

need you   now. _____ And I   don't know how __ I can

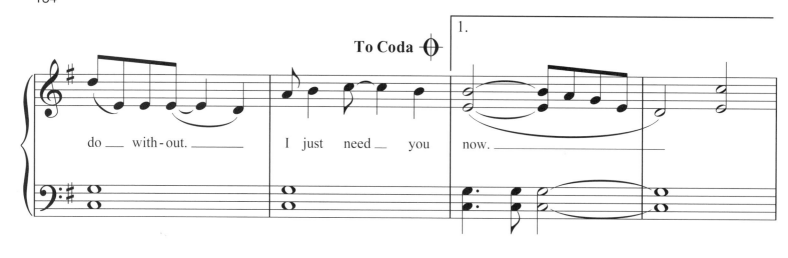

To Coda

do — with-out. _____ I just need _ you now. _____

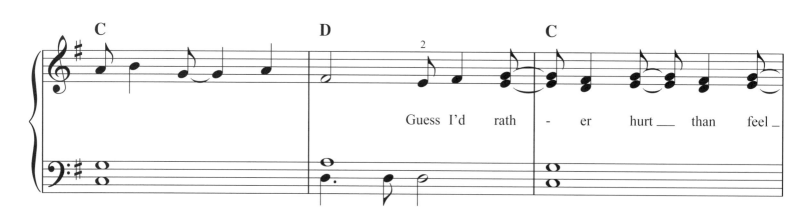

Em

2.

Em   **D**   **G**

An -   now. _____

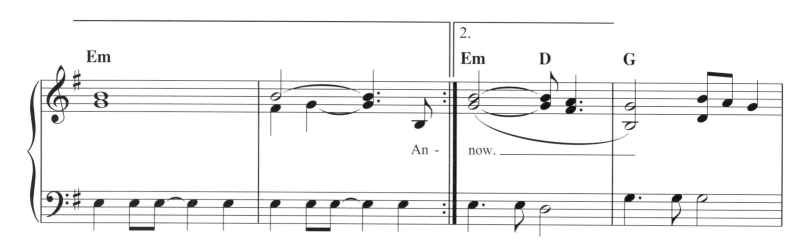

C   **D**   **C**

Guess I'd rath - er hurt _ than feel _

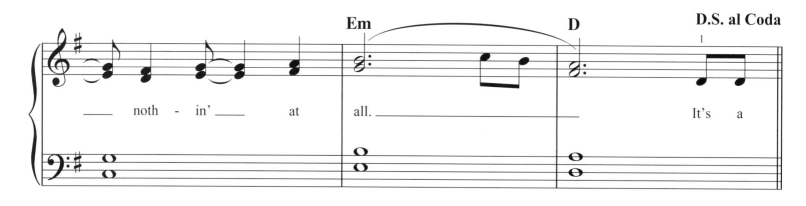

Em   **D**   **D.S. al Coda**

_ noth - in' _ at all.   It's a

now _____

I just need ___ you now. _____ Oh, ___

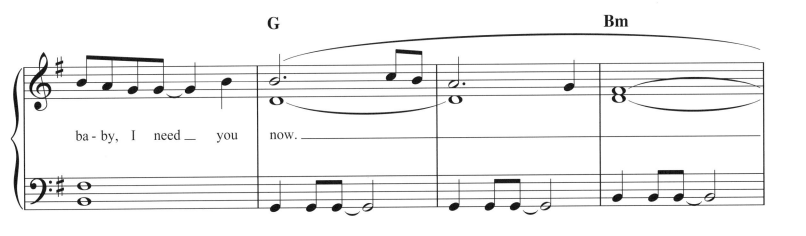

ba - by, I need ___ you now. _____

SEA OF LOVE

Words and Music by GEORGE KHOURY
and PHILIP BAPTISTE

With a slow Rock beat

Do you re- mem- ber ___ when ___ we met? ___
Come with me ___ my ___ love ___

That's the day ___ I knew you were my pet.
to the sea, ___ the sea ___ of ___ love.

I ___ want to tell you just how much ___ I

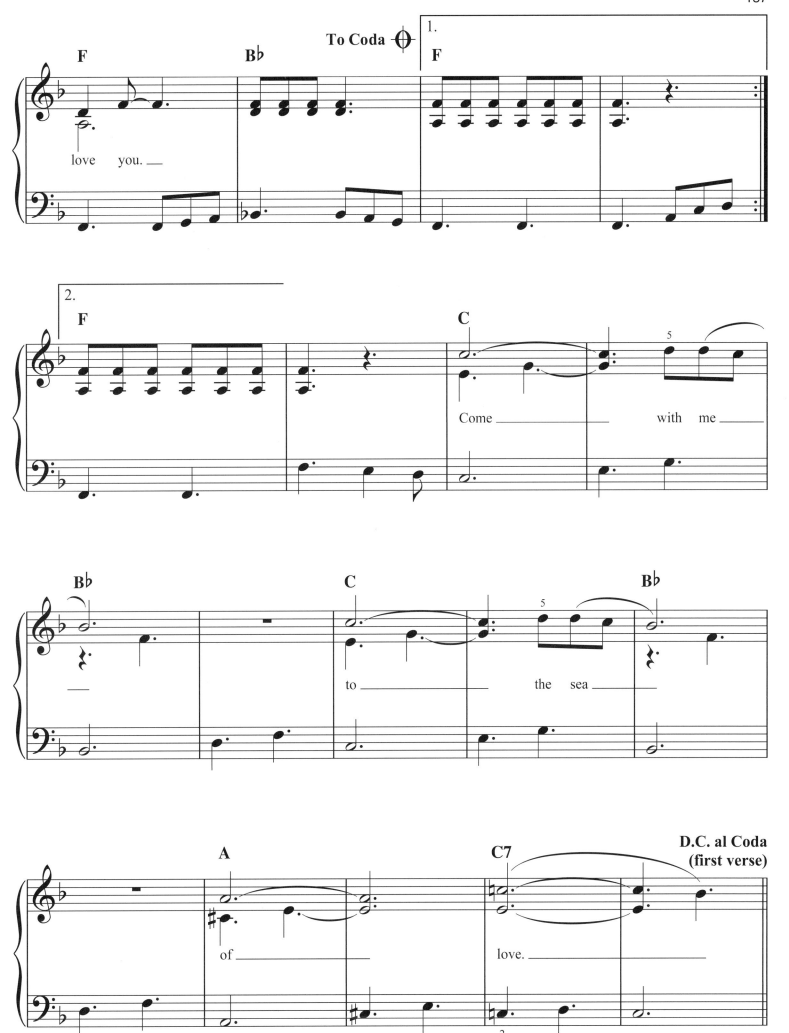

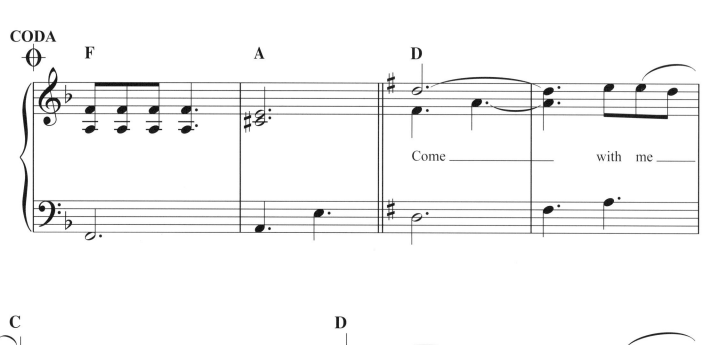

CODA

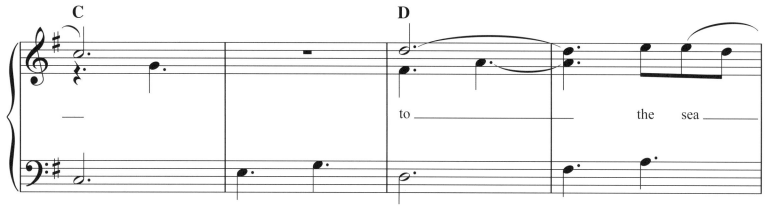

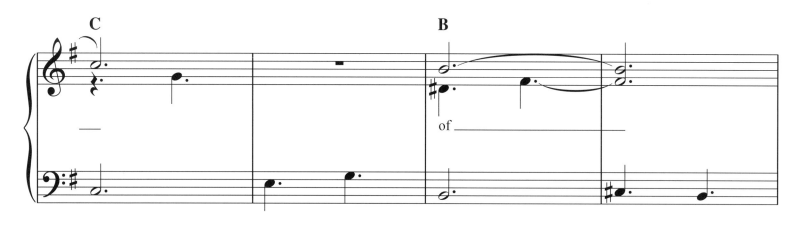

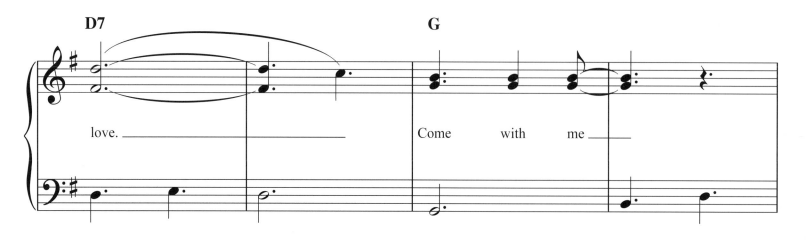

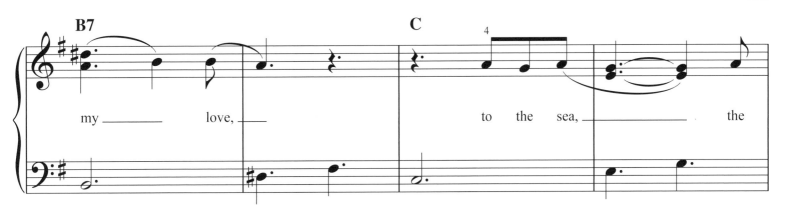

my _____ love, _____   to the sea, _____ the

sea ____ of love. ____   I _____ want to tell you
I _____ want to tell you

just how ___ much I love you. ___
oh, how ___ much I love you. ___

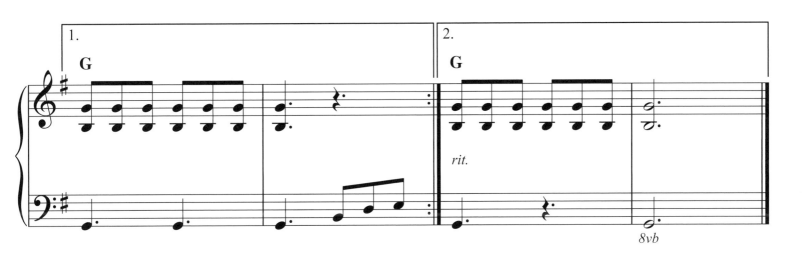

SHE WILL BE LOVED

Words and Music by ADAM LEVINE
and JAMES VALENTINE

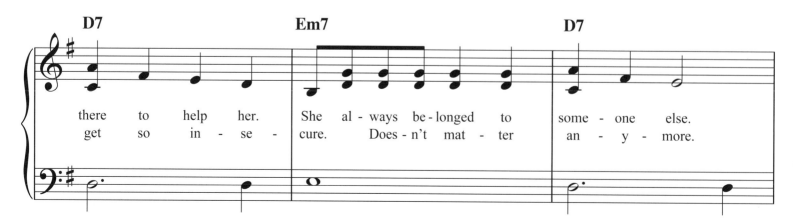

141

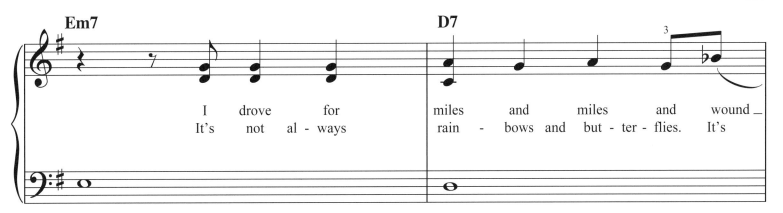

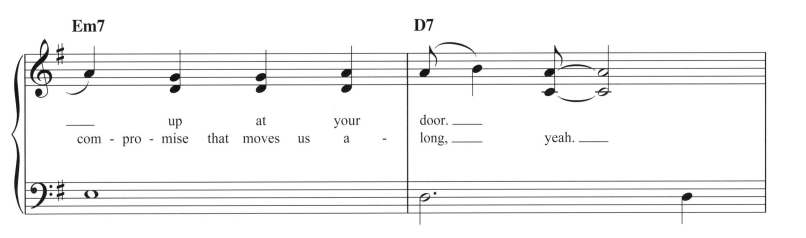

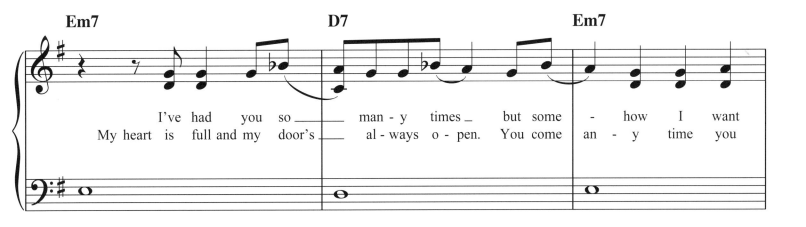

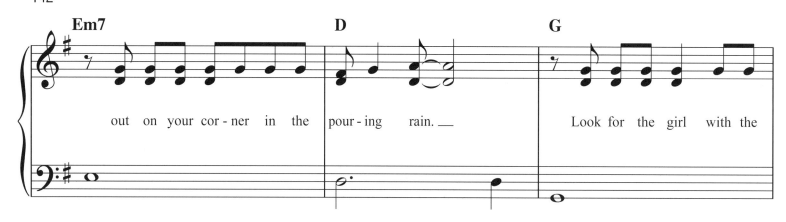

out on your cor-ner in the pour-ing rain.____ Look for the girl with the

bro - ken smile._____ Ask her if she wants to stay a while __ and she

will be loved._____ And she will be

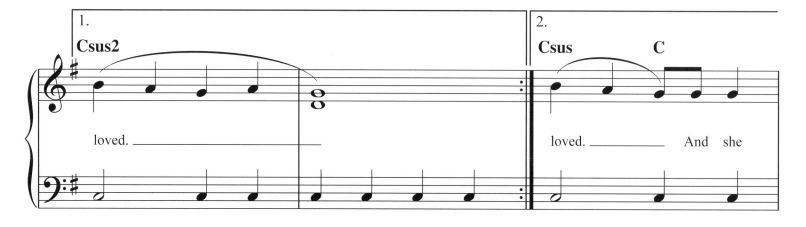

1. loved._____

2. loved._____ And she

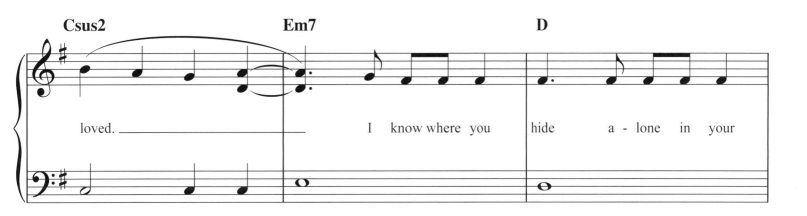

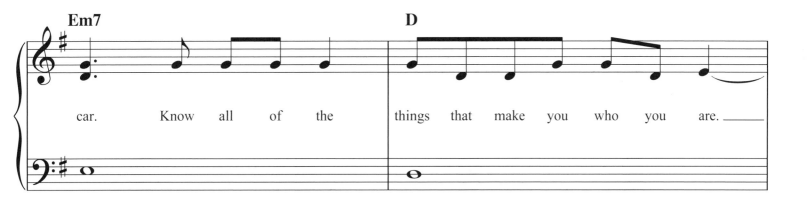

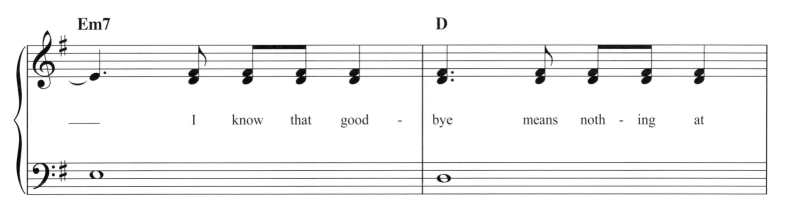

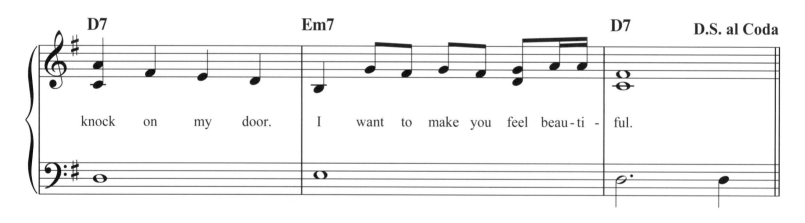

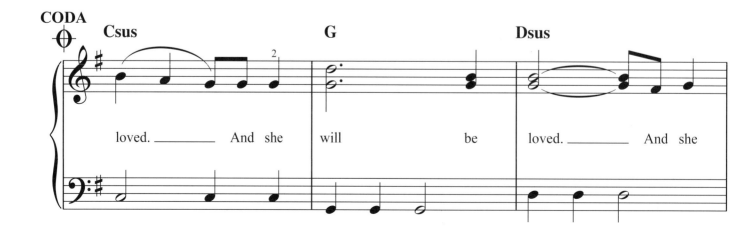

will   be   loved. _____   Please   don't

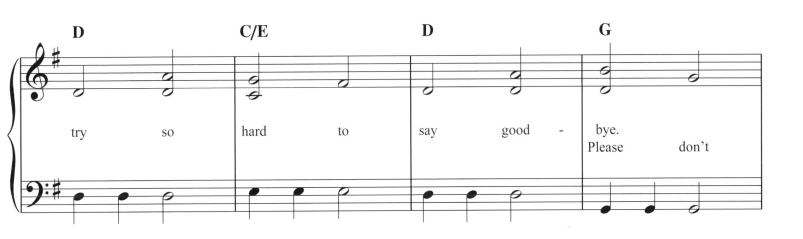

try   so   hard   to   say   good - bye. Please don't

try   so   hard   to   say   good - bye. Please don't

try   so   hard   to   say   good - bye.

SHE'S ALWAYS A WOMAN

Words and Music by
BILLY JOEL

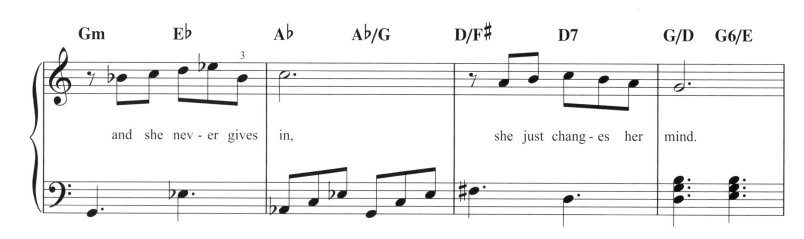

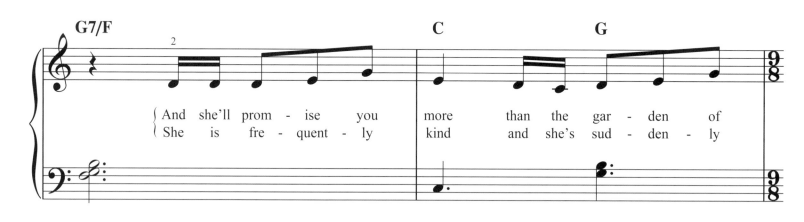

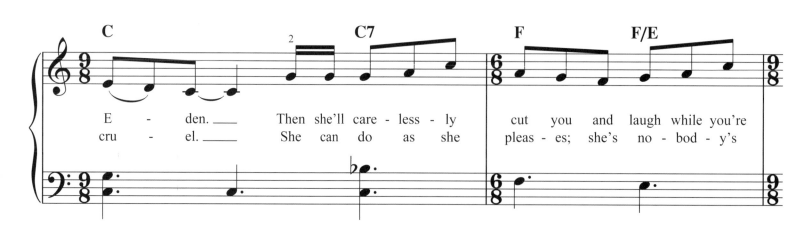

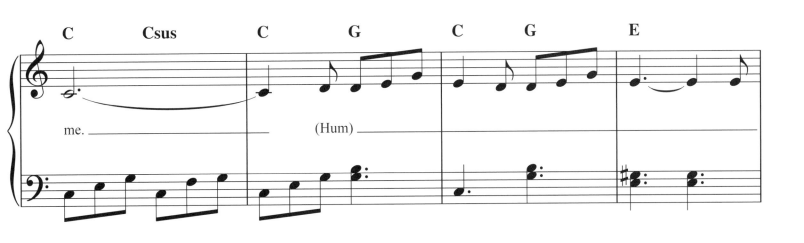

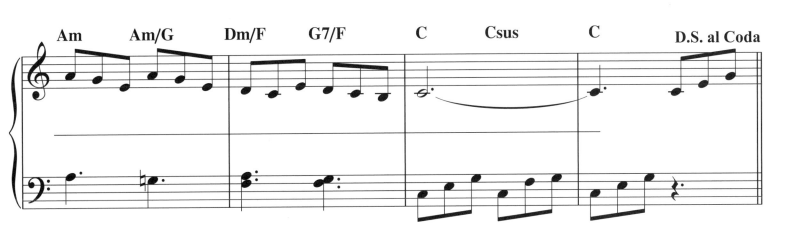

CODA

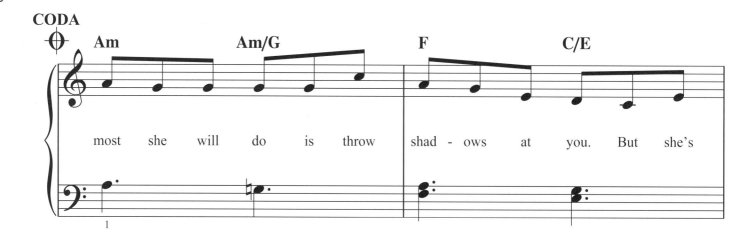

Am   Am/G   F   C/E

most she will do is throw shad - ows at you. But she's

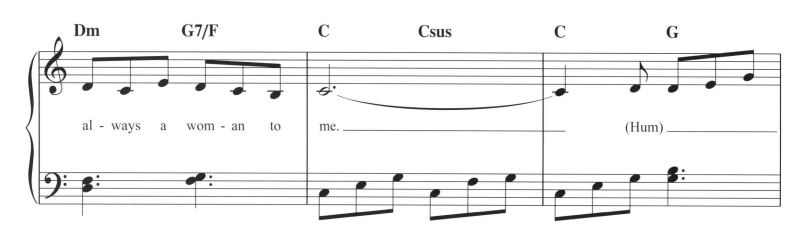

Dm   G7/F   C   Csus   C   G

al - ways a wom - an to me. _____ (Hum) _____

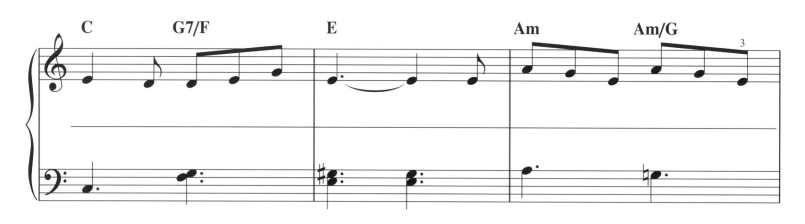

C   G7/F   E   Am   Am/G

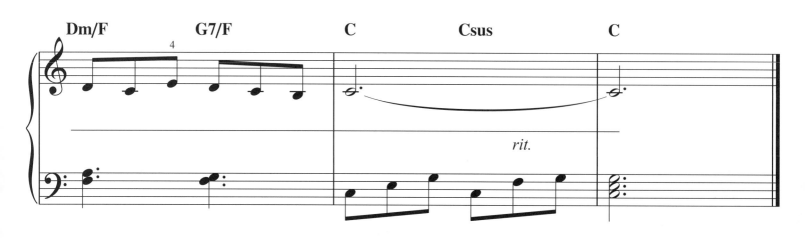

Dm/F   G7/F   C   Csus   C

rit.

STRANGERS IN THE NIGHT

Words by CHARLES SINGLETON and EDDIE SNYDER
Music by BERT KAEMPFERT

Moderately slow

Stran - gers in the night _____ ex - chang - ing glanc - es,

won-d'ring in the night _____ what were the chanc - es we'd be shar-ing love _____

_____ be - fore the night was through. _____

Some-thing in your eyes ____ was so in - vit - ing, some-thing in your smile ____

____ was so ex - cit - ing, some-thing in my heart ____ told me I must have

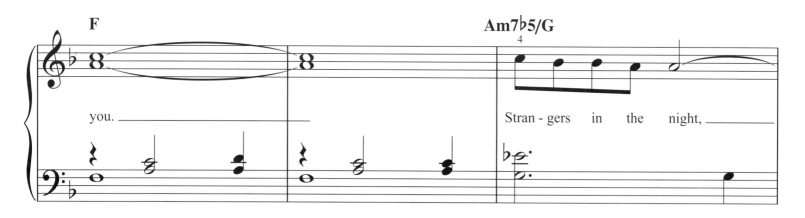

you. ____ Stran - gers in the night, ____

____ two lone - ly peo - ple, we were stran-gers in the night ____ up to the mo-ment when we

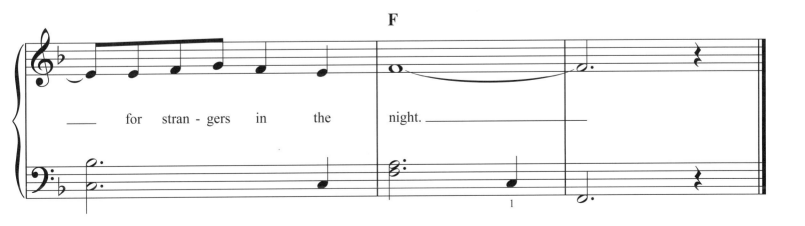

SOMEONE LIKE YOU

Words and Music by ADELE ADKINS
and DAN WILSON

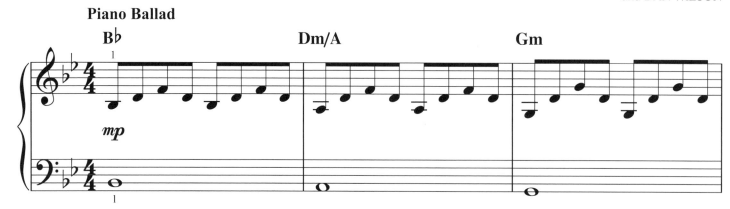

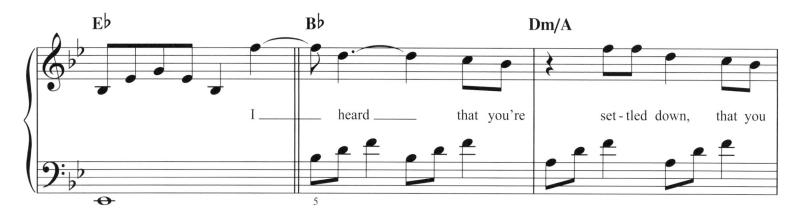

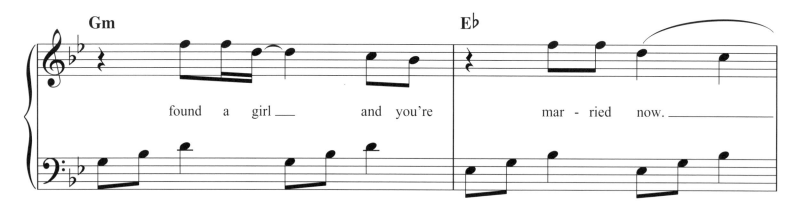

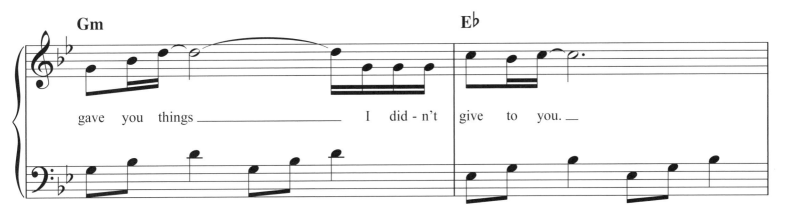

Gm ... **Eb** ...

gave you things _____ I did - n't give to you. __

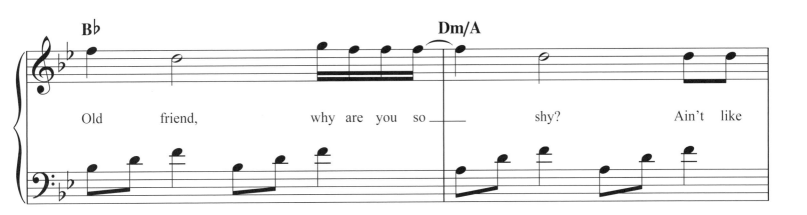

Bb ... **Dm/A** ...

Old friend, why are you so __ shy? Ain't like

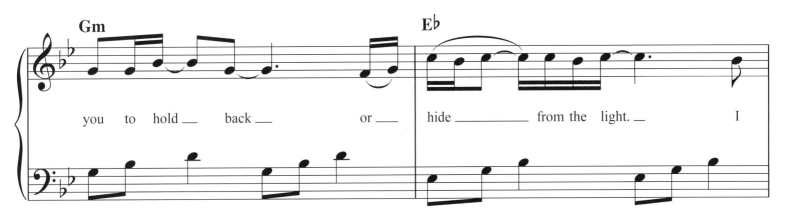

Gm ... **Eb** ...

you to hold __ back __ or __ hide _____ from the light. __ I

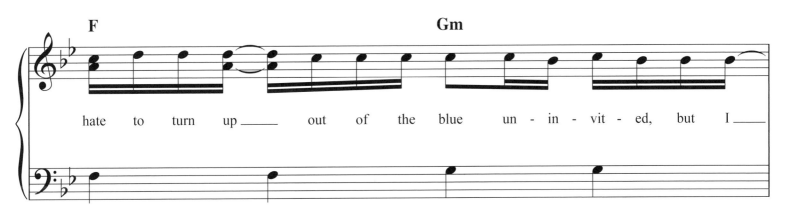

F ... **Gm** ...

hate to turn up ____ out of the blue un - in - vit - ed, but I ____

could-n't stay a - way, _____ I could-n't fight it. I had

hoped you'd see my face and that you'd be re - mind - ed that, for

me, _____ it is - n't o - ver. _____

Nev - er mind, _ I'll find some - one like you. I wish

nothing but ___ the best for you, too. Don't for-

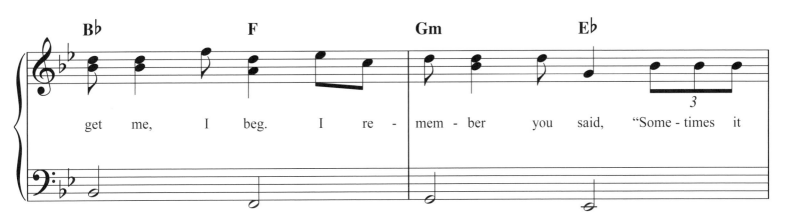

get me, I beg. I re - mem - ber you said, "Some - times it

To Coda ⊕

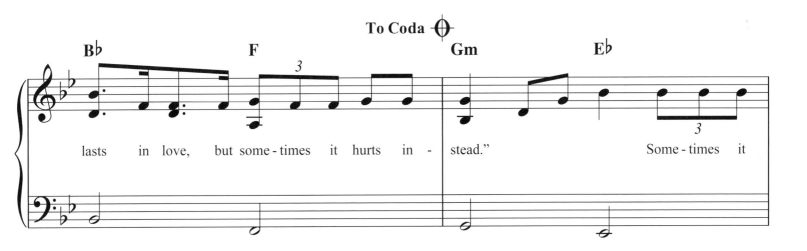

lasts in love, but some - times it hurts in - stead." Some - times it

lasts in love, but some - times it hurts in - stead. ___

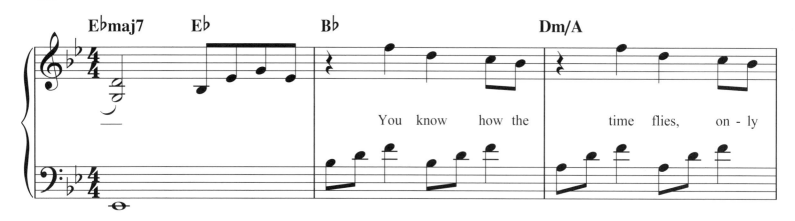

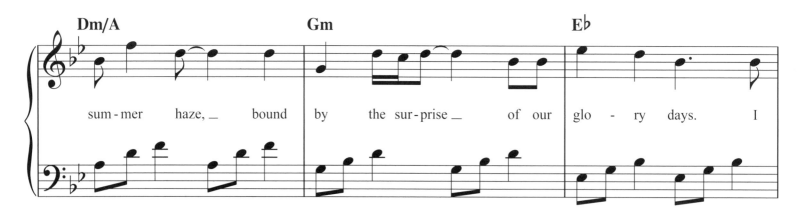

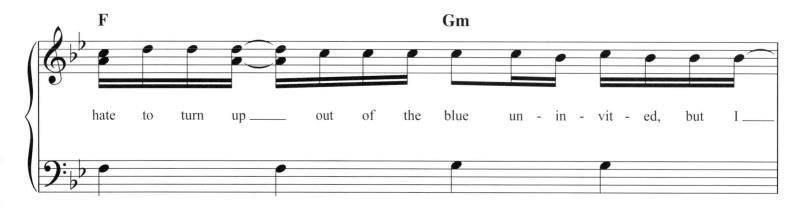

Eb

___ could - n't stay a - way, _____ I could - n't fight it. I had

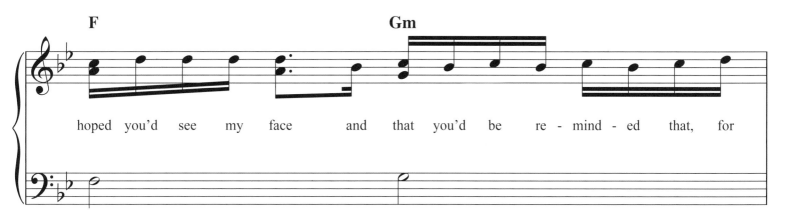

F   Gm

hoped you'd see my face   and that you'd be re - mind - ed that, for

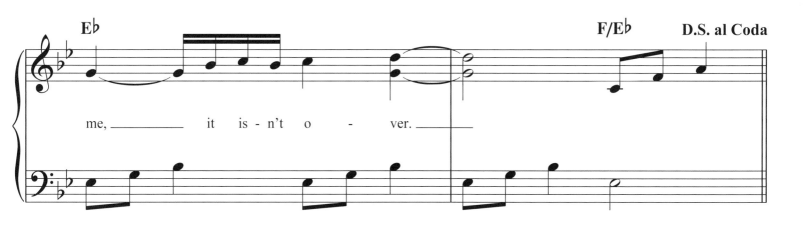

Eb   F/Eb   D.S. al Coda

me, _____ it is - n't o - ver. _____

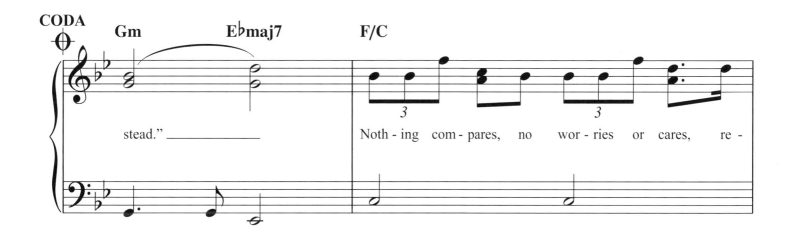

CODA

Gm   Ebmaj7   F/C

stead." _____   Noth - ing com - pares, no wor - ries or cares, re -

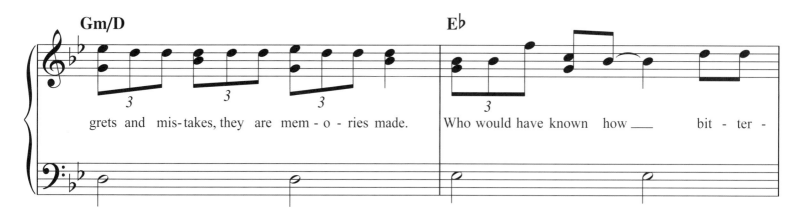

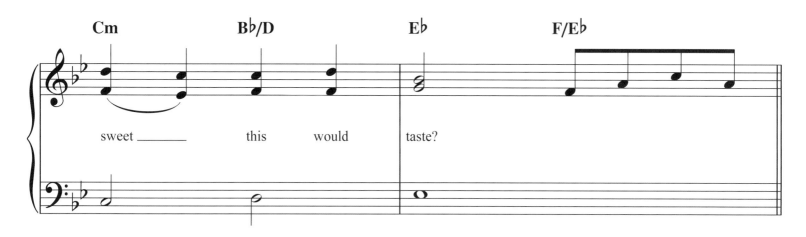

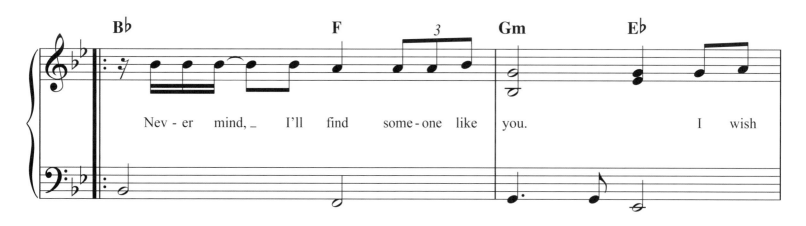

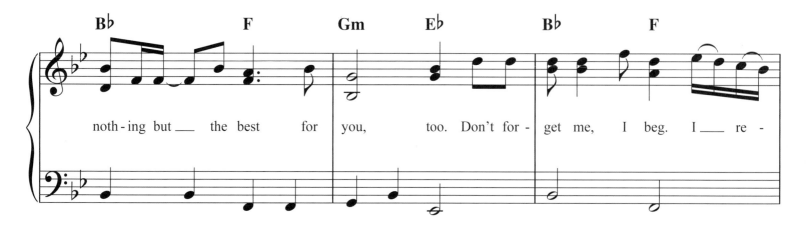

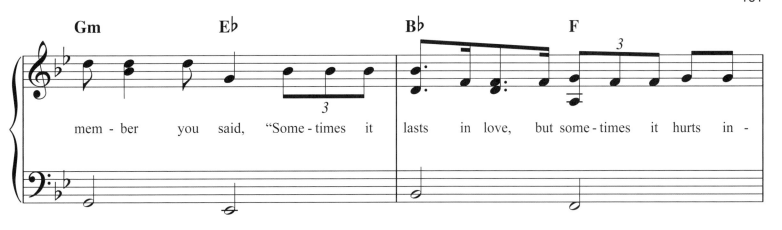

mem - ber you said, "Some - times it lasts in love, but some - times it hurts in -

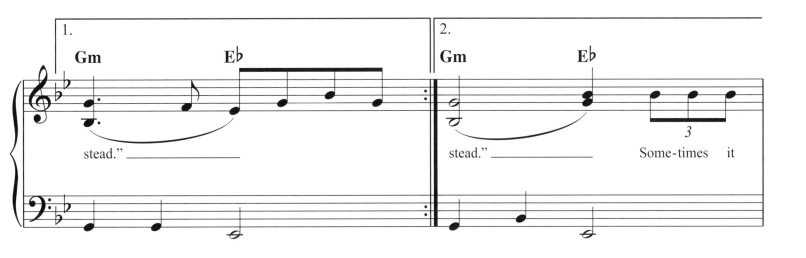

1.
stead." _____

2.
stead." _____ Some - times it

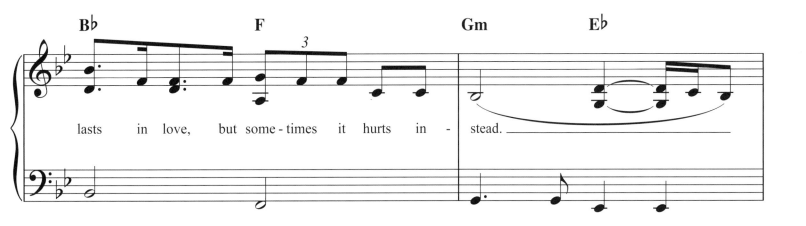

lasts in love, but some - times it hurts in - stead. _____

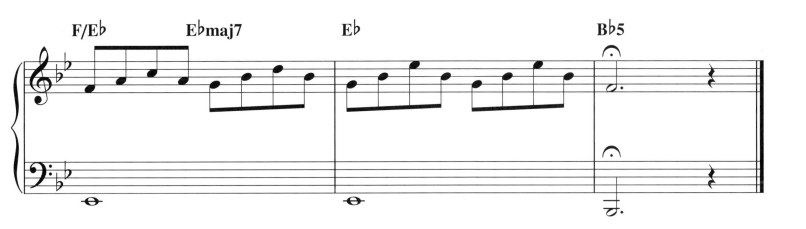

STILL THE ONE

Words and Music by JOHN HALL
and JOHANNA HALL

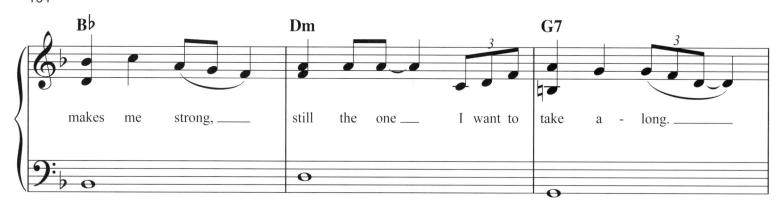

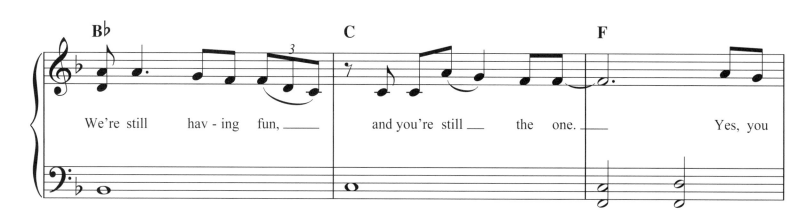

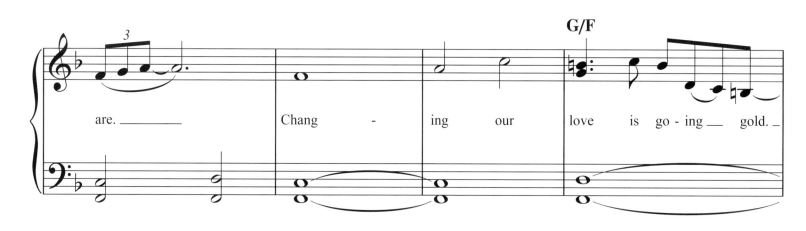

Ooh, _____ you're still the one _____ I love to touch, _____

still the one _ and I can't get e - nough. _____ We're still hav - ing fun, _____

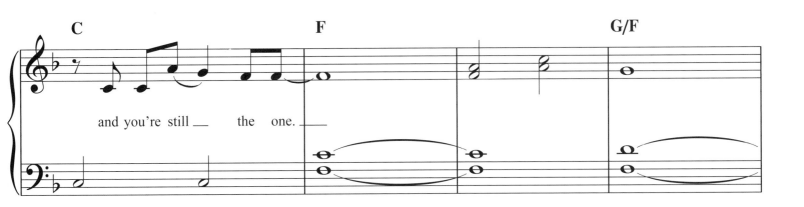

and you're still _ the one. _____

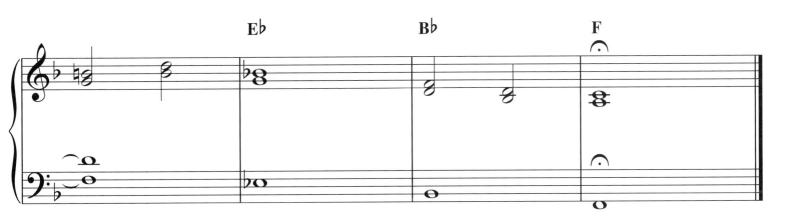

THINKING OUT LOUD

Words and Music by ED SHEERAN
and AMY WADGE

When your legs don't work like they used to be-fore
When my hair's all gone and my mem - o - ry fades

and I can't sweep you off of your feet,
and the crowds don't re - mem - ber my name.

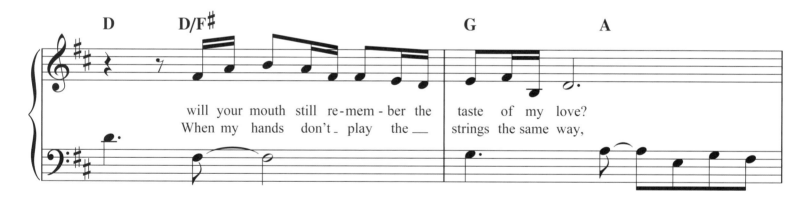

will your mouth still re-mem-ber the taste of my love?
When my hands don't play the ___ strings the same way,

Will your eyes still smile from your cheeks? And dar - ling, I
I know you will still love me the same. 'Cause, hon - ey, your

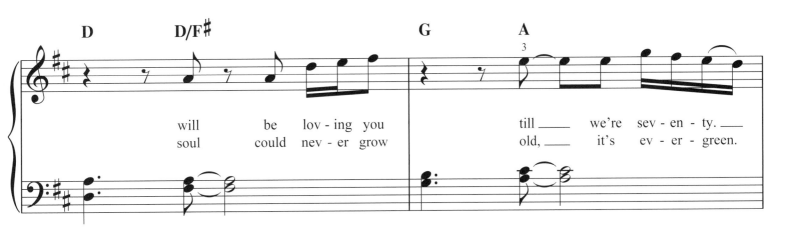

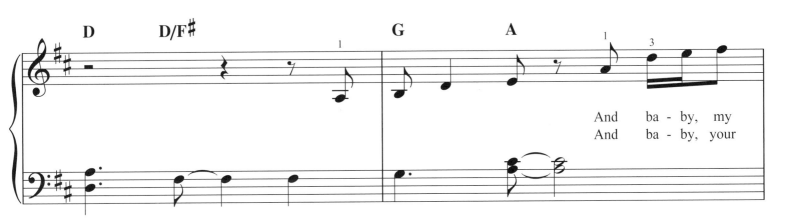

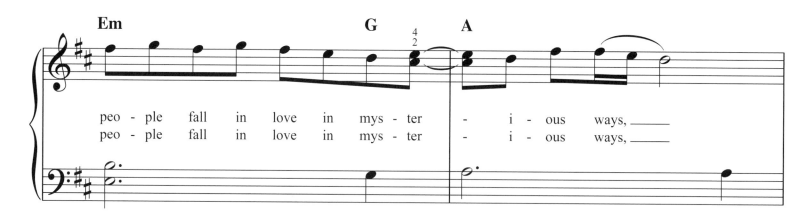

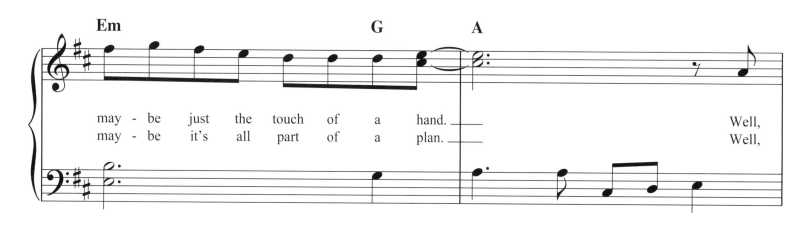

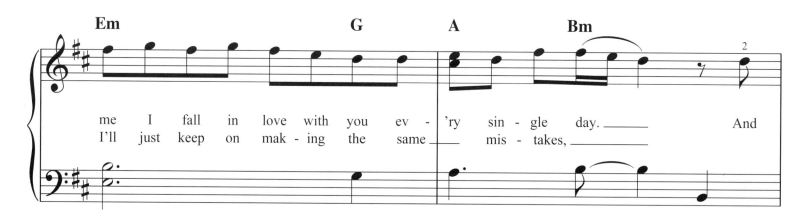

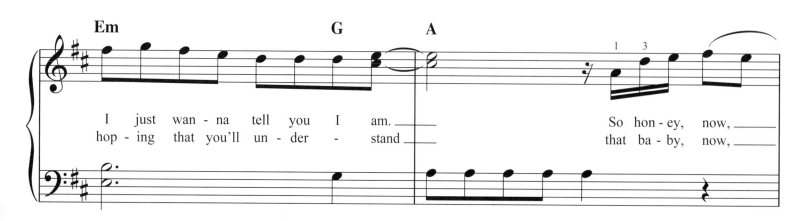

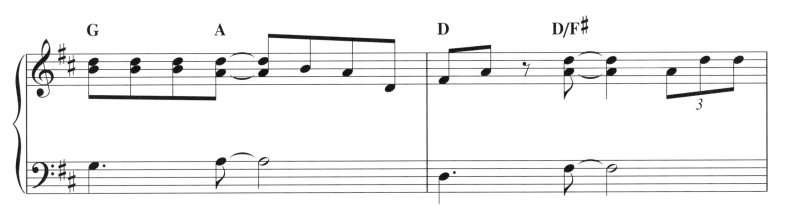

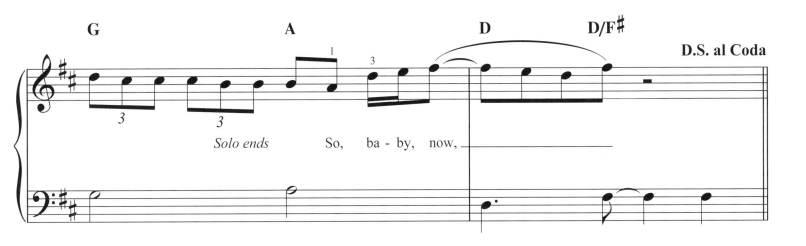

D.S. al Coda

Solo ends   So, ba - by, now,

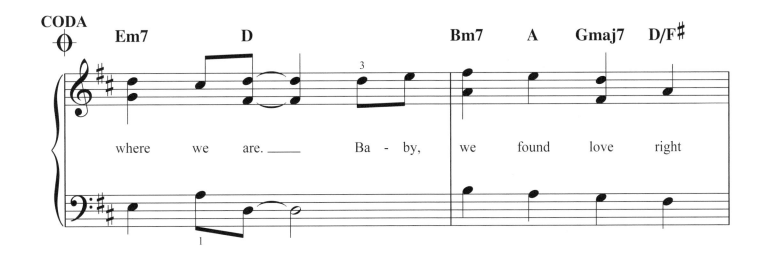

where   we   are.   Ba - by,   we   found   love   right

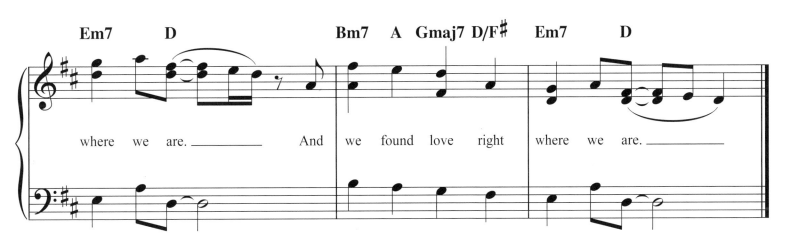

where   we   are.   And   we   found   love   right   where   we   are.

A THOUSAND YEARS

from the Summit Entertainment film THE TWILIGHT SAGA: BREAKING DAWN – Part 1

Words and Music by DAVID HODGES
and CHRISTINA PERRI

Moderately, in one

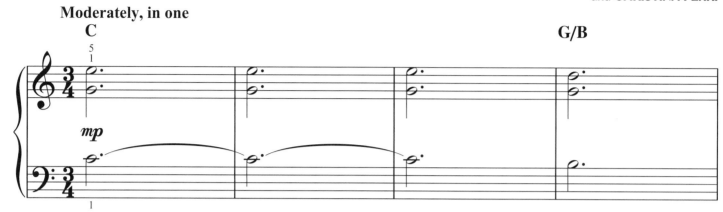

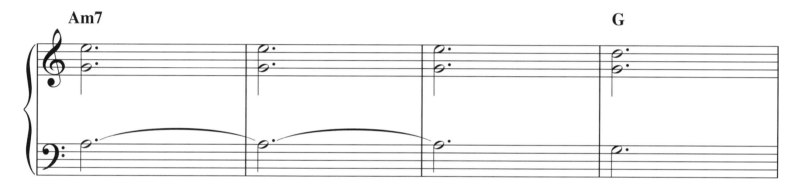

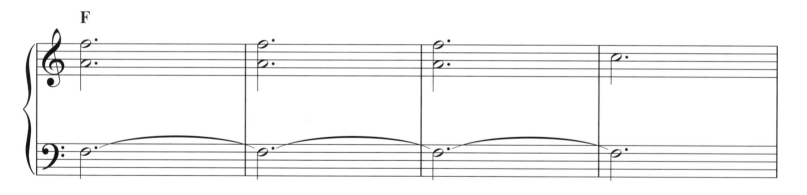

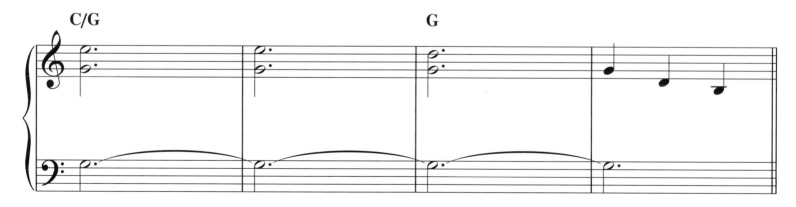

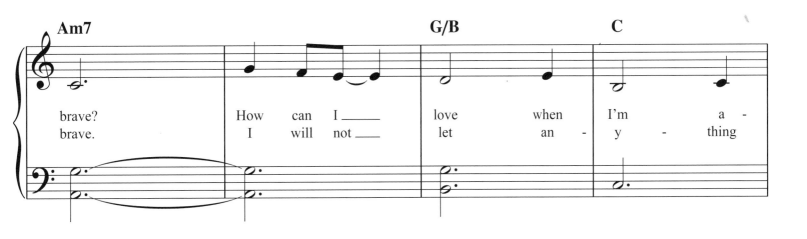

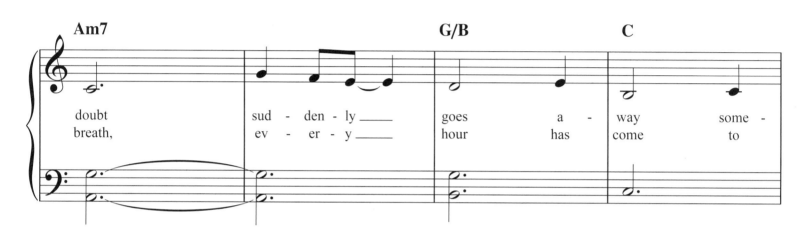

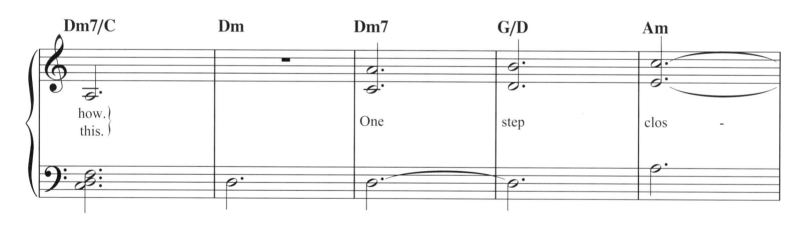

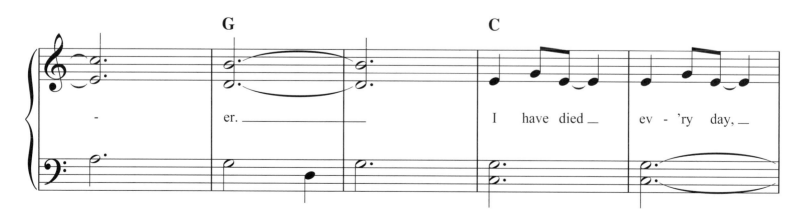

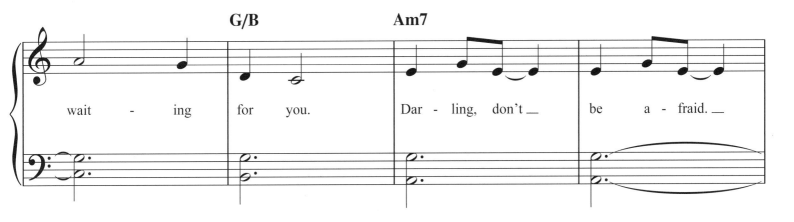

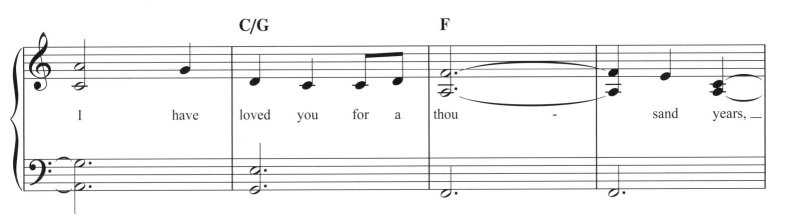

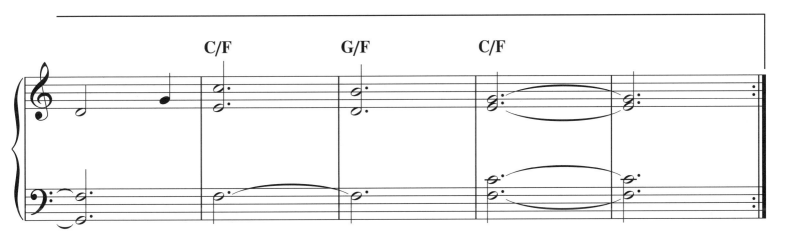

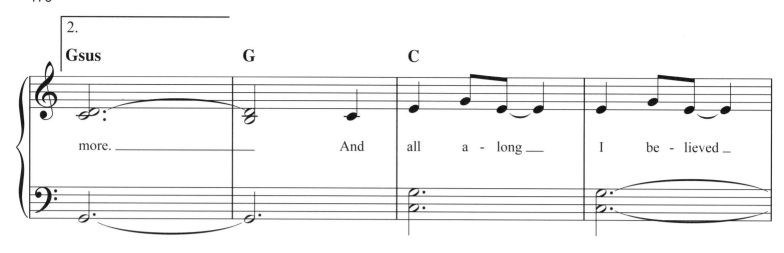

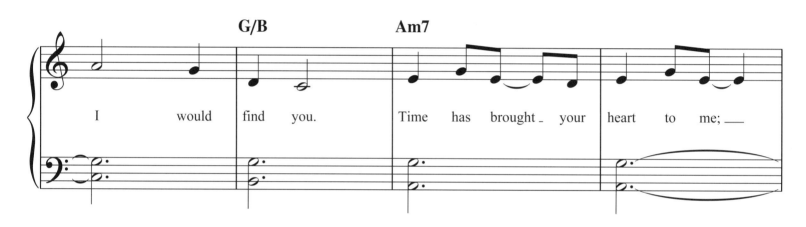

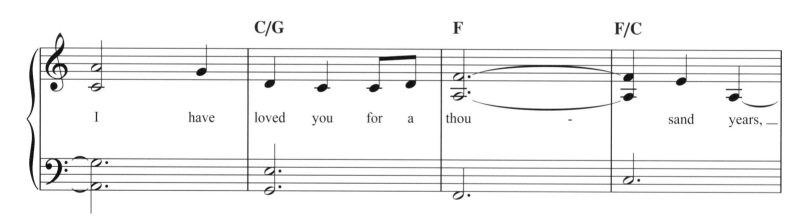

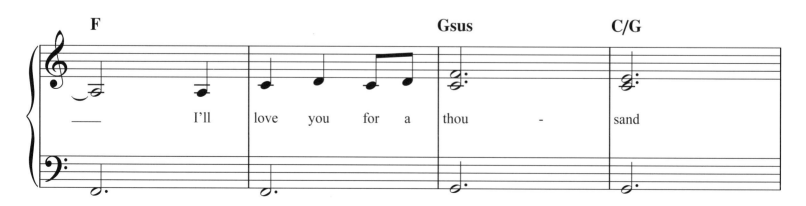

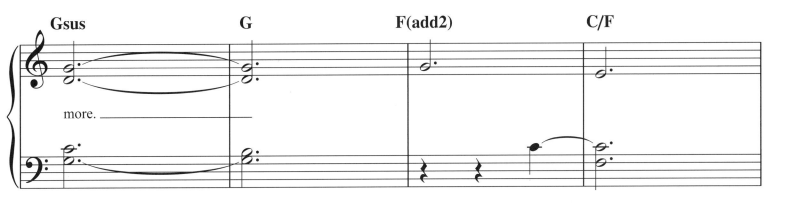

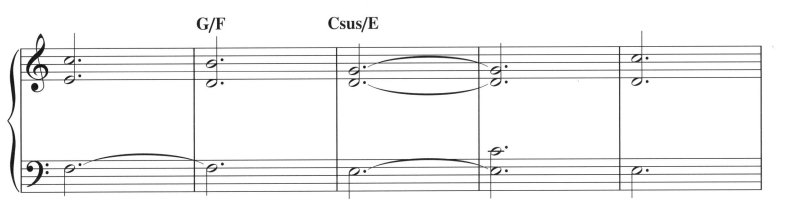

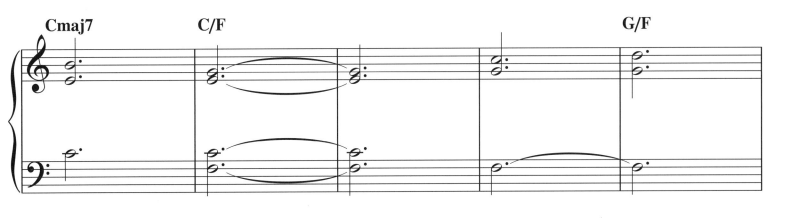

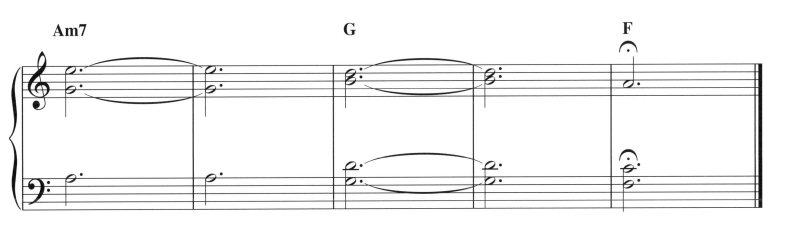

TRUE LOVE WAYS

Words and Music by NORMAN PETTY
and BUDDY HOLLY

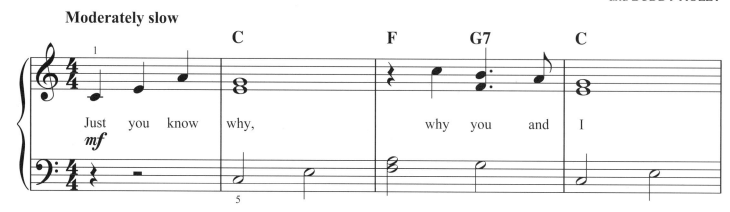

Moderately slow

Just you know why, why you and I

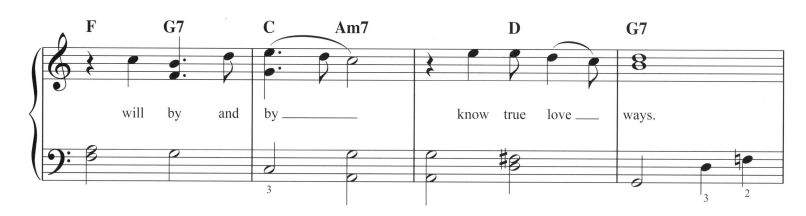

will by and by _____ know true love ___ ways.

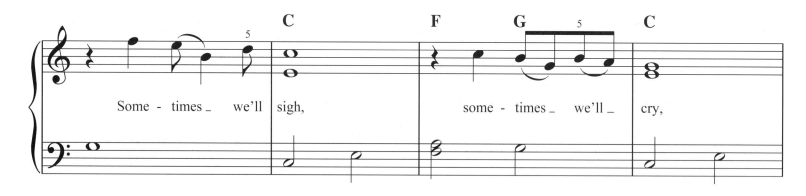

Some - times _ we'll sigh, some - times _ we'll _ cry,

and we'll know why, just you and I know true _ love _ ways.

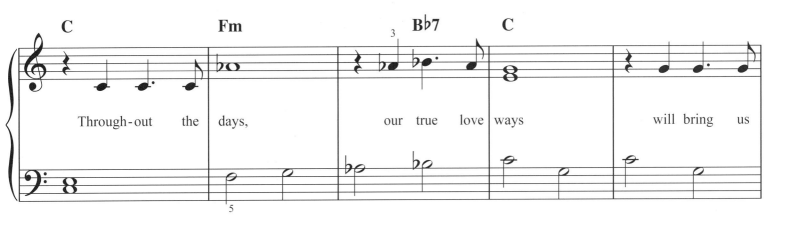

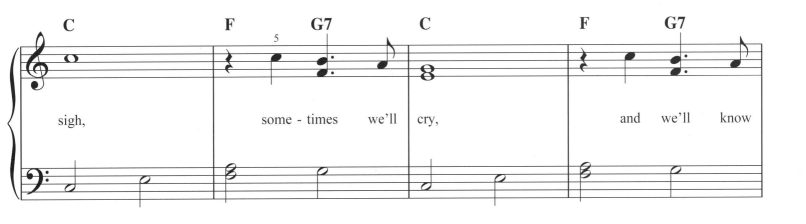

UNCONDITIONALLY

Words and Music by KATY PERRY,
LUKASZ GOTTWALD, MAX MARTIN
and HENRY WALTER

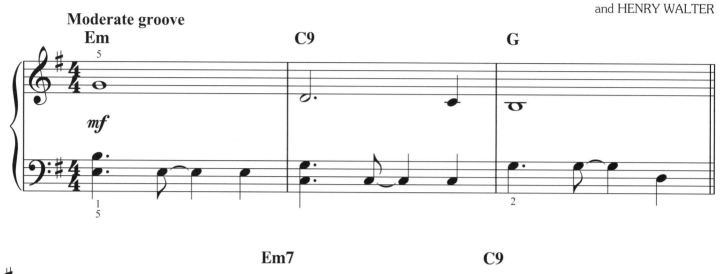

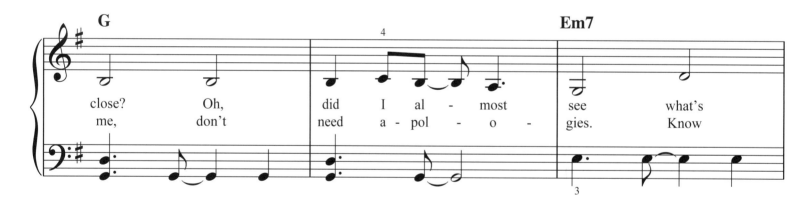

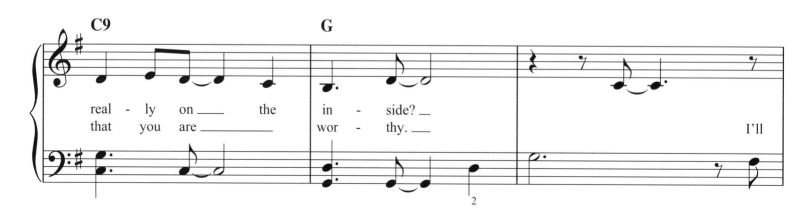

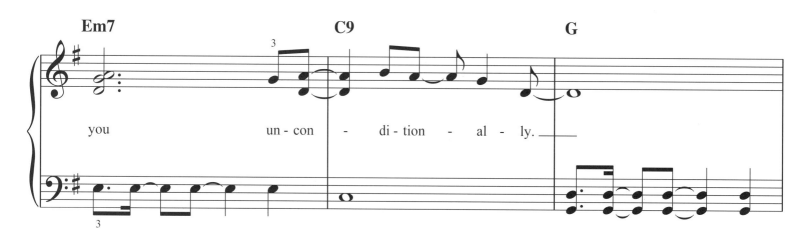

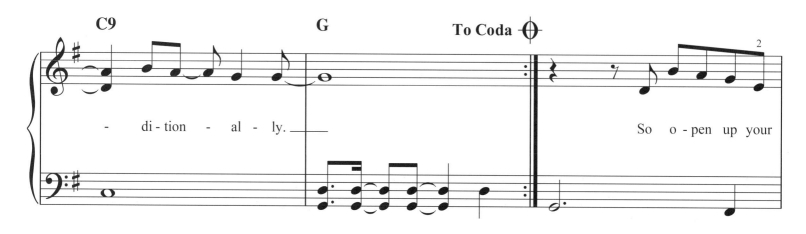

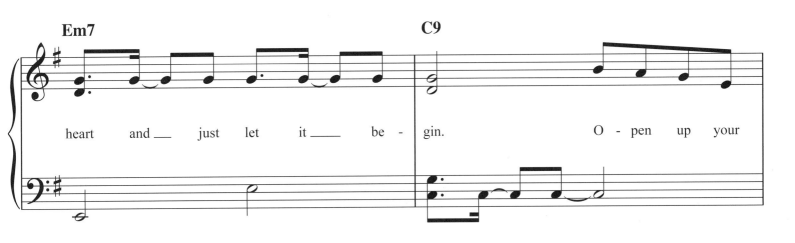

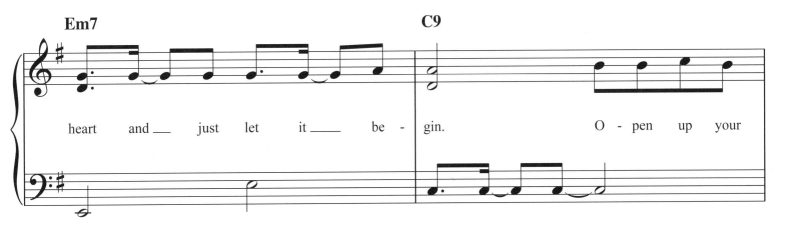

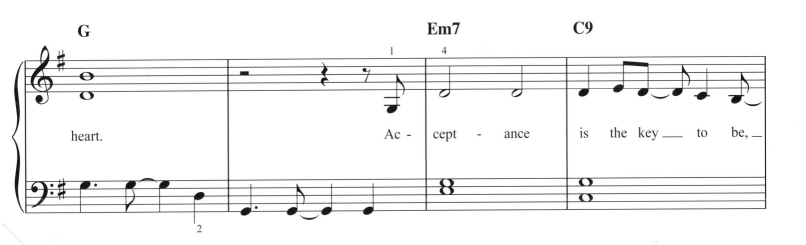

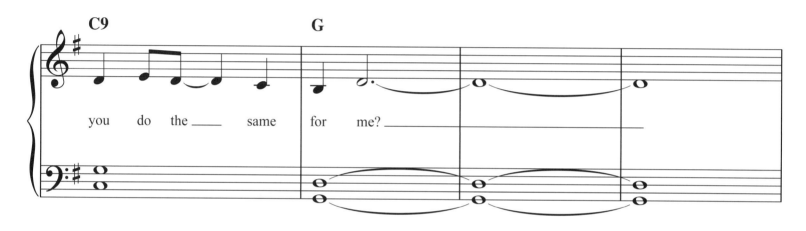

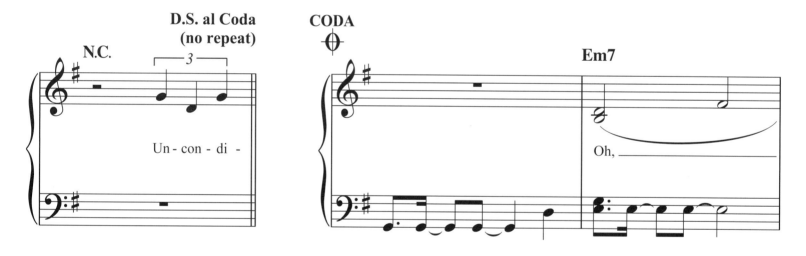

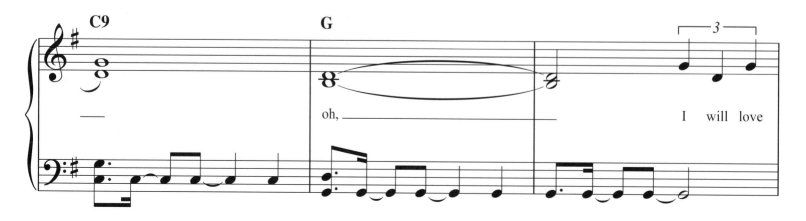

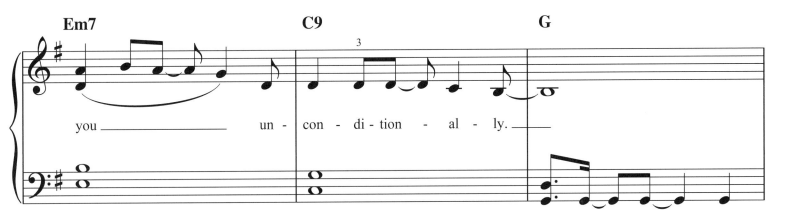

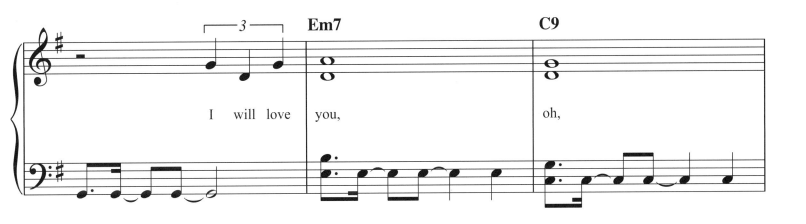

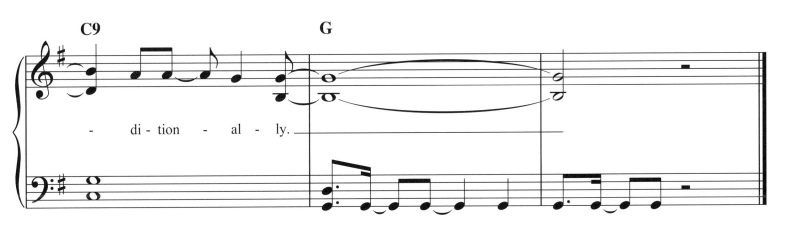

The Way You Look Tonight

from SWING TIME

Words by DOROTHY FIELDS
Music by JEROME KERN

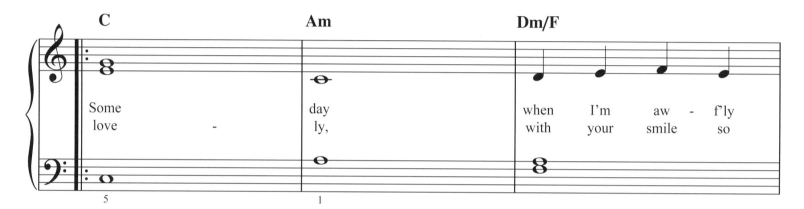

C7/E — you
F6 — and the way you
G7 — look to -

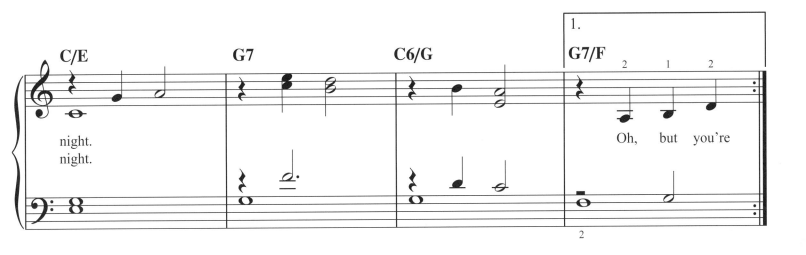

C/E — night.
G7
C6/G
1. **G7/F** — Oh, but you're

night.

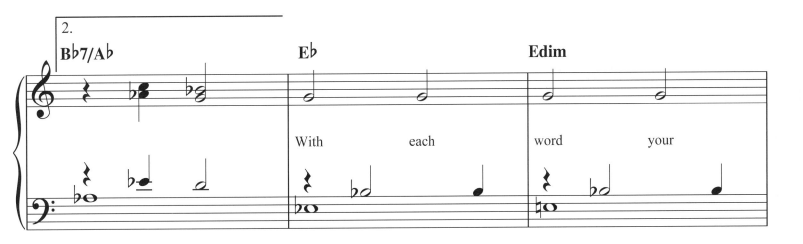

2. **B♭7/A♭**
E♭ — With each
Edim — word your

Fm7 — ten - der - ness
B♭7/F — grows,
E♭/G — tear - ing my fear

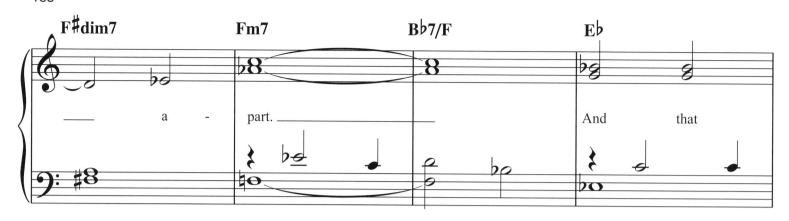

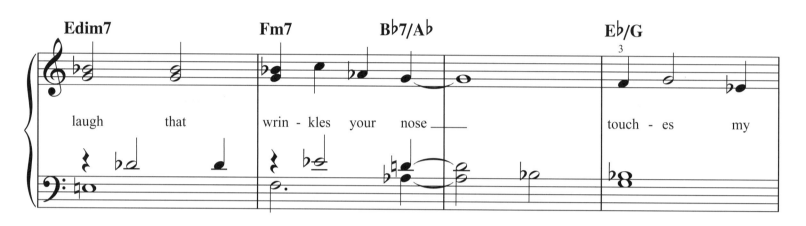

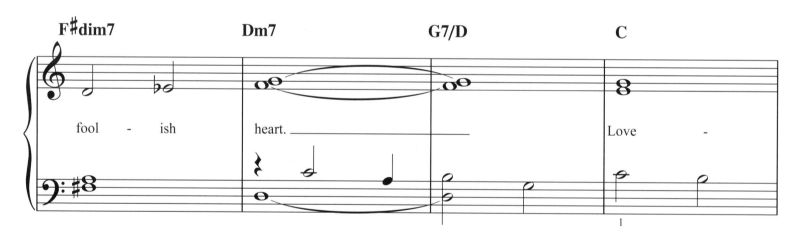

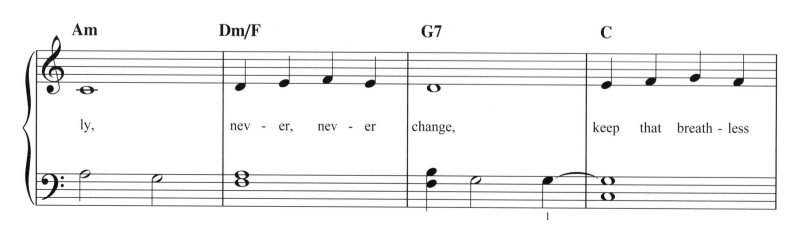

189

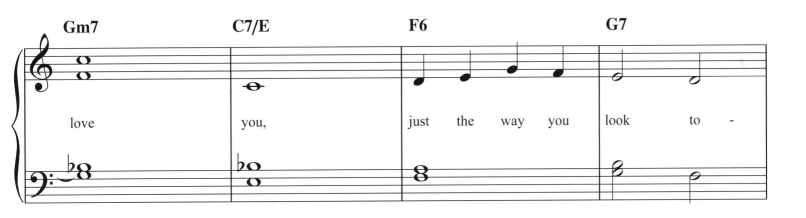

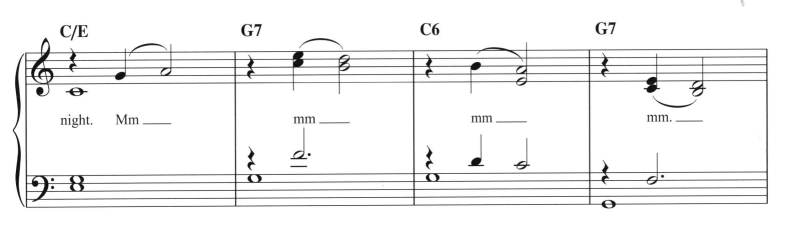

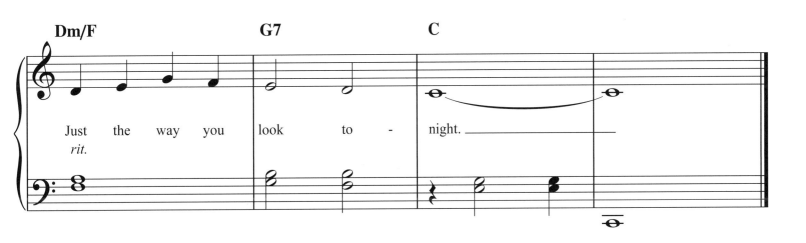

WHEN YOU SAY NOTHING AT ALL

Words and Music by DON SCHLITZ
and PAUL OVERSTREET

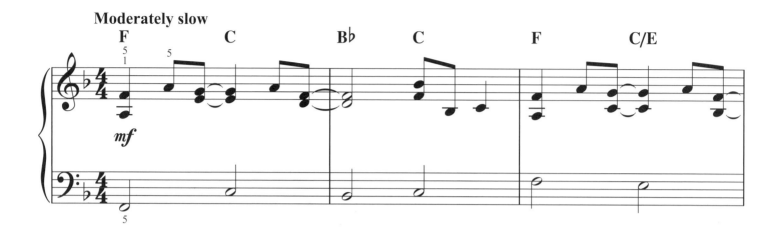

It's a-maz - ing how you can speak right __ to my heart. __
All day long __ I can hear peo - ple talk - ing out loud. __

With-out say - ing a word,
But when you __ hold me near,

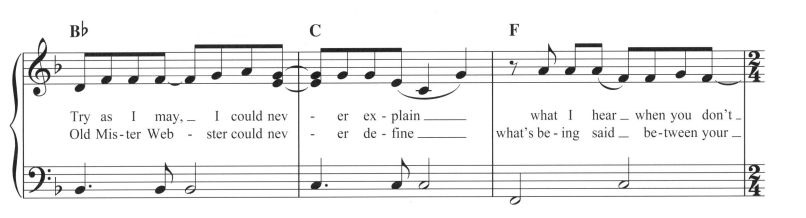

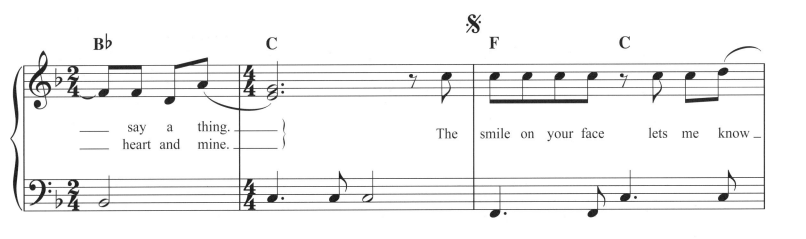

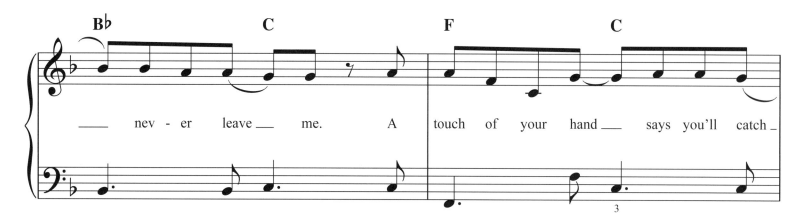

nev - er leave ___ me.   A   touch of your hand ___ says you'll catch ___

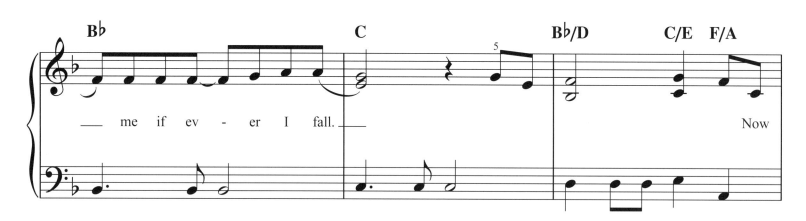

___ me if ev - er I fall. ___   Now

you say it best _____   when you say noth - ing at all. ___

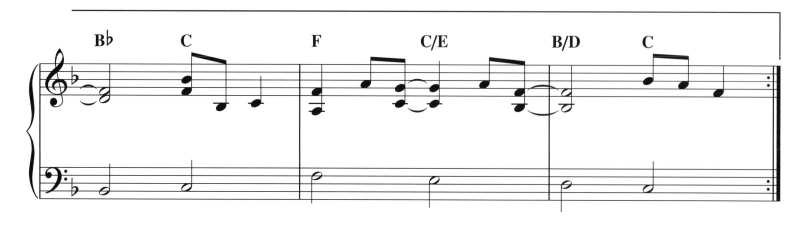

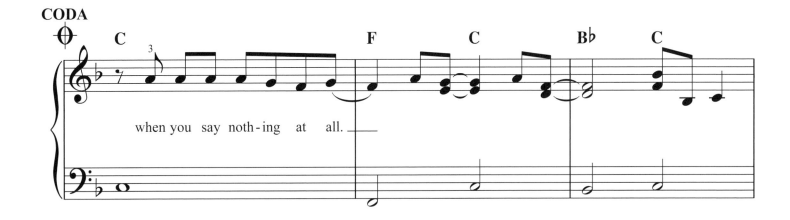

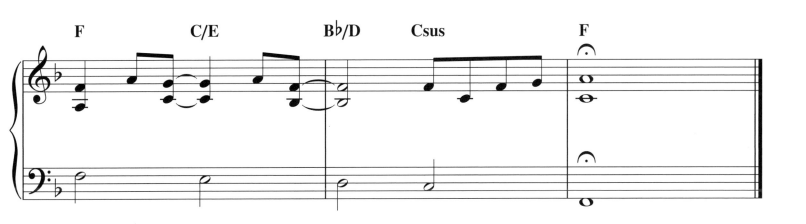

YOU ARE THE SUNSHINE OF MY LIFE

Words and Music by
STEVIE WONDER

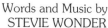

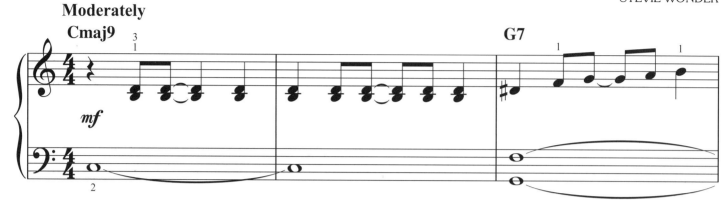

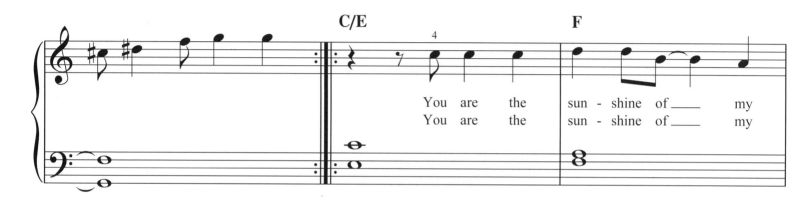

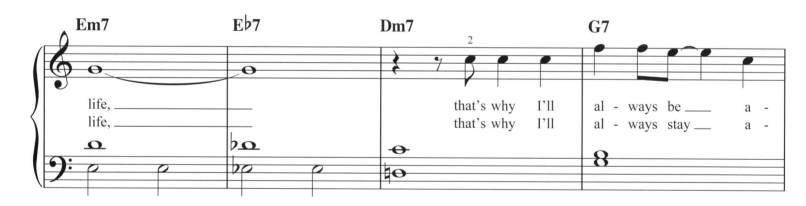

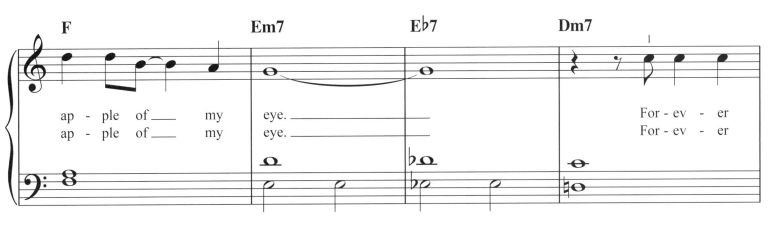

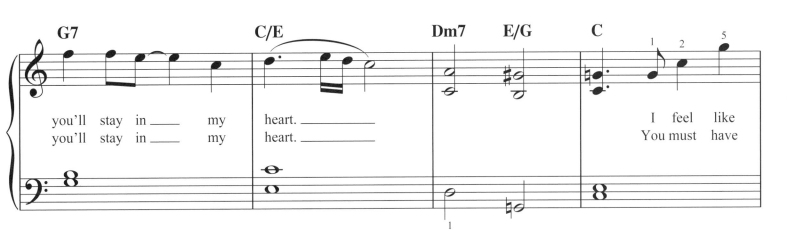

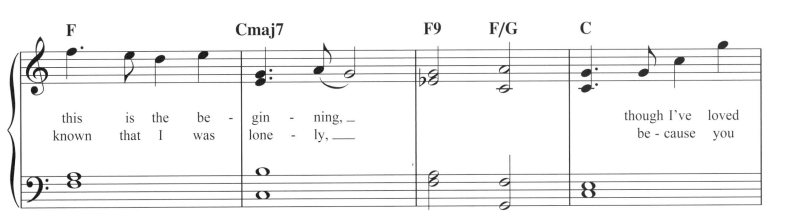

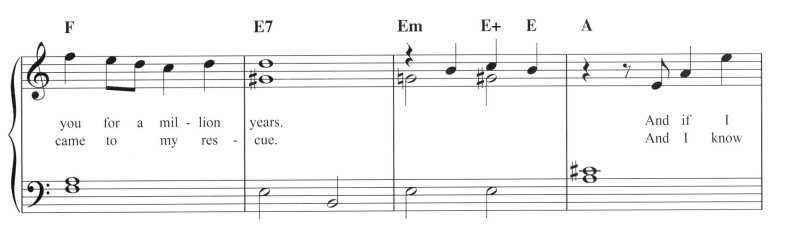

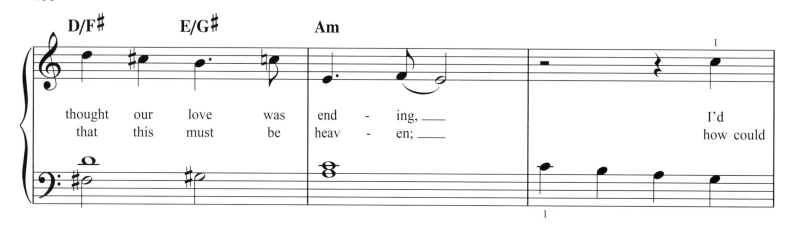

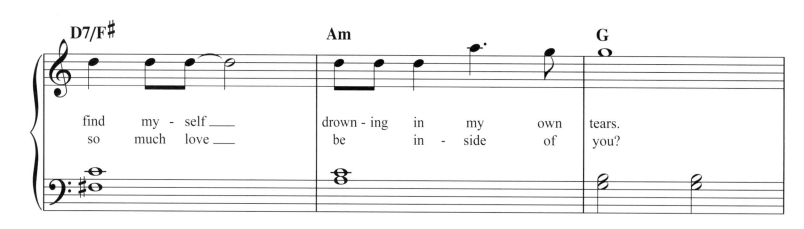

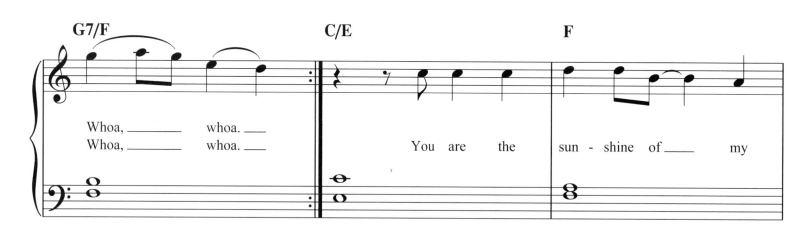

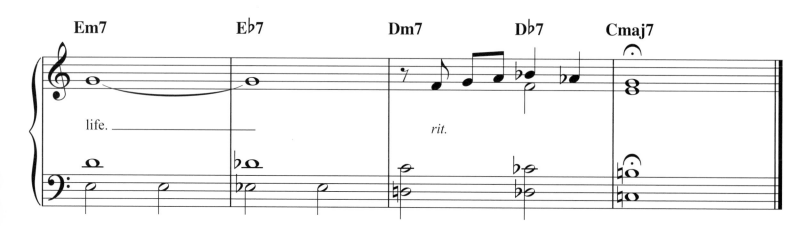

WITH OR WITHOUT YOU

Words and Music by U2

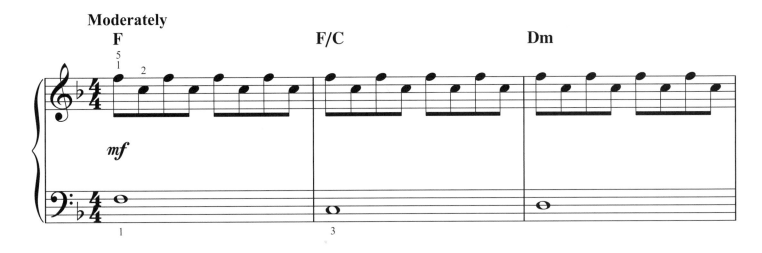

Moderately

See the stone ___ set in your eyes.

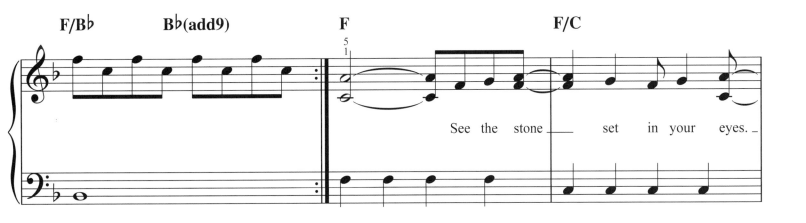

See the thorn ___ twist in your side. ___ I'll wait

198

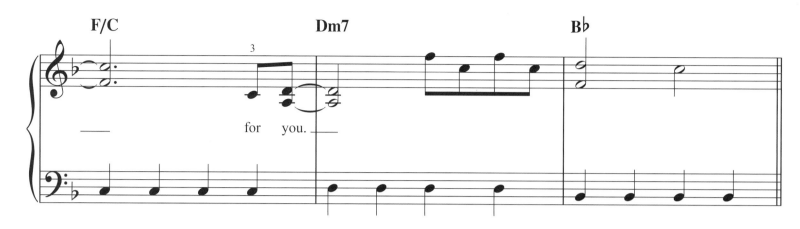

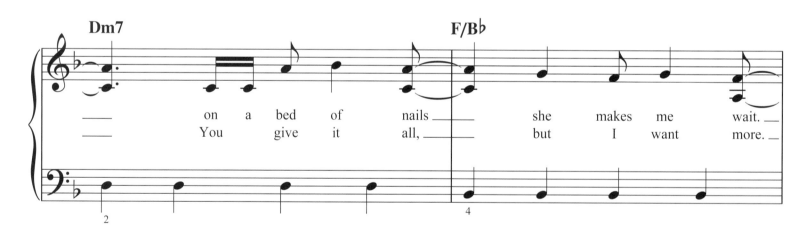

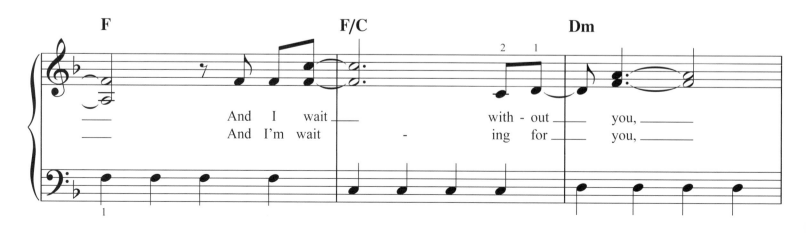

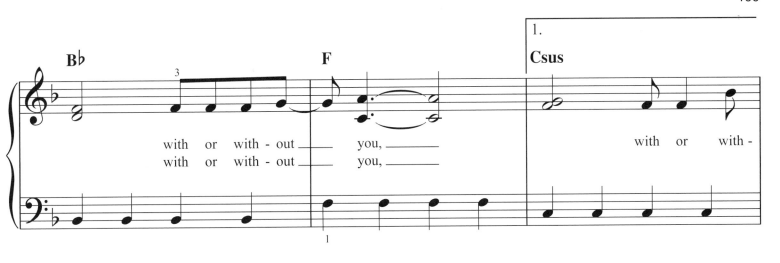

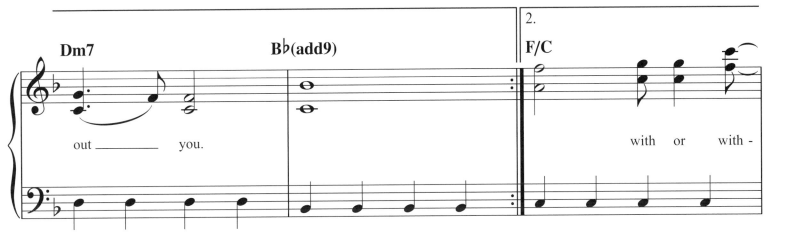

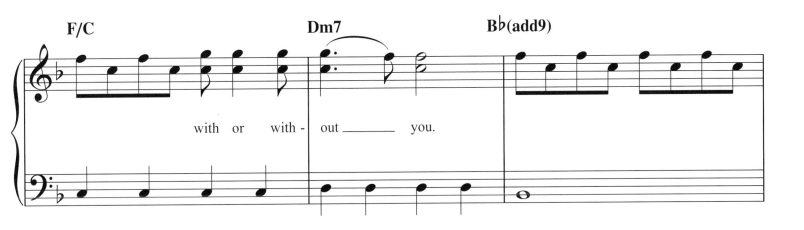

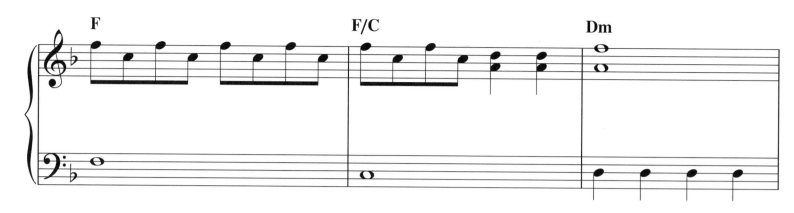

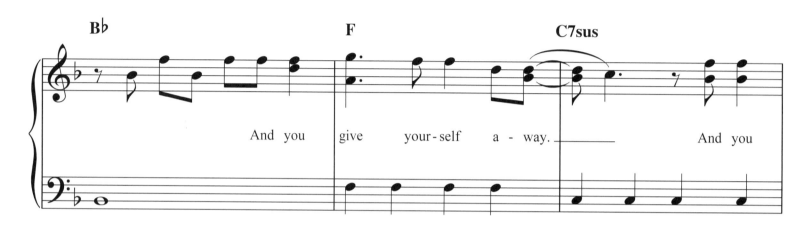

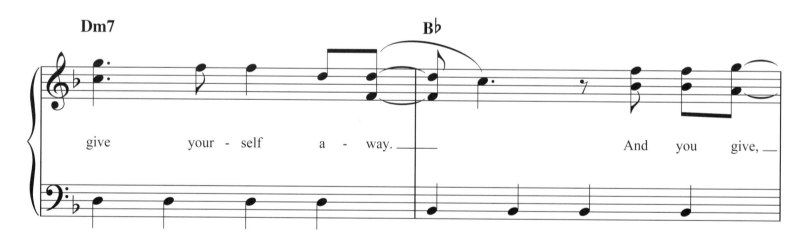

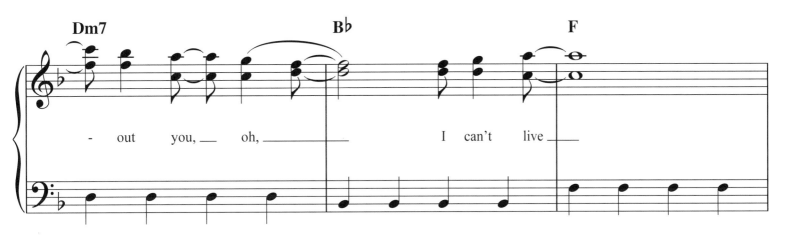

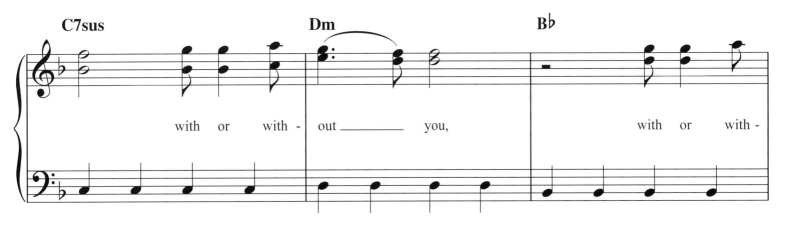

YOU ARE THE REASON

Words and Music by CALUM SCOTT,
COREY SANDERS and JONATHAN MAGUIRE

There goes my heart beat-ing,

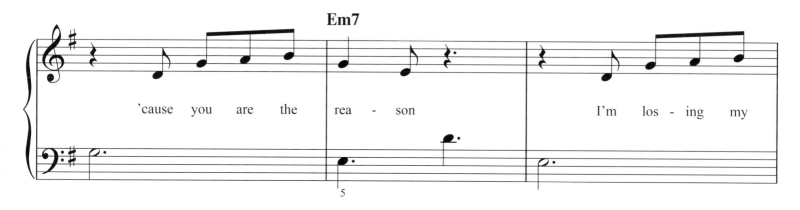

'cause you are the rea-son   I'm los-ing my

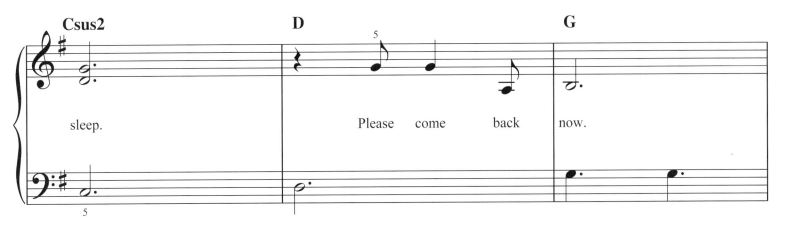

Csus2 — sleep.
D — Please come back
G — now.

There goes my mind rac - ing, and you are the

Em — rea - son that I'm still **Csus2** breath - ing.

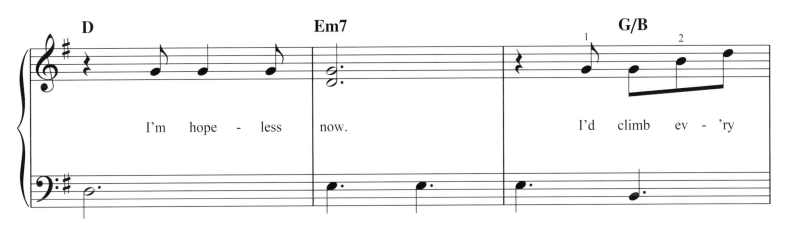

D — I'm hope - less **Em7** now. **G/B** I'd climb ev - 'ry

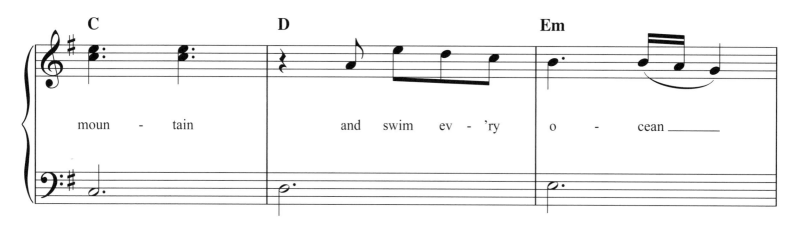

moun - tain   and swim ev - 'ry   o - cean _____

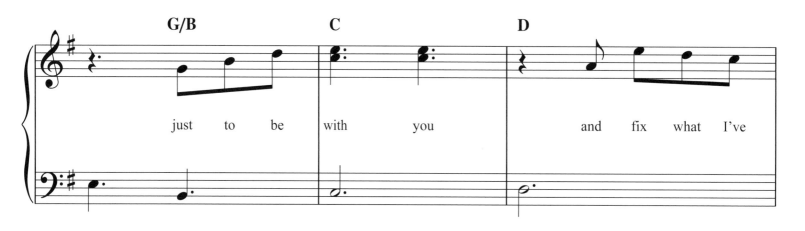

just   to   be   with   you   and   fix   what   I've

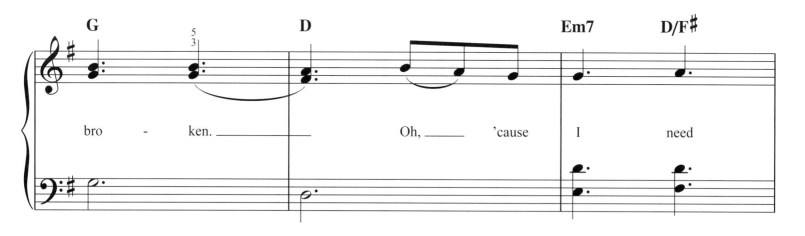

bro - ken. _____   Oh, _____ 'cause   I   need

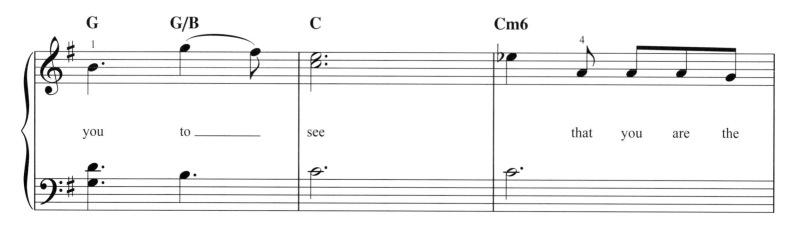

you   to _____   see   that   you   are   the

rea - son. ___

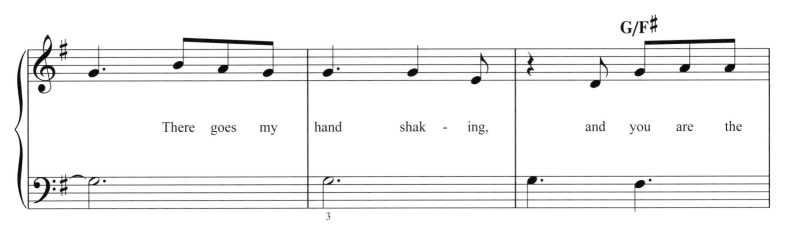

G/F#

There goes my hand shak - ing, and you are the

Em7 **C**

rea - son my heart keeps bleed - ing.

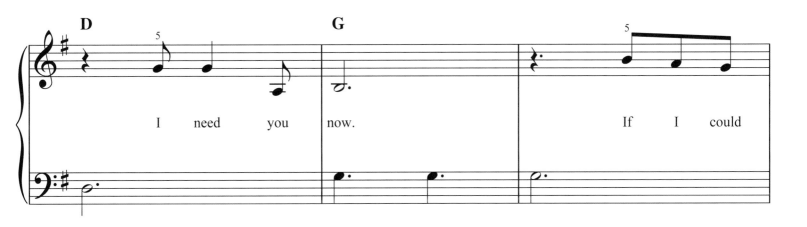

D **G**

I need you now. If I could

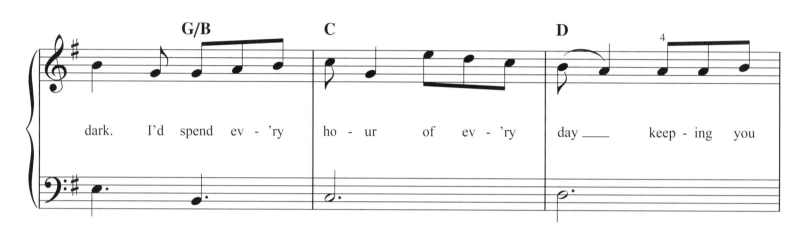

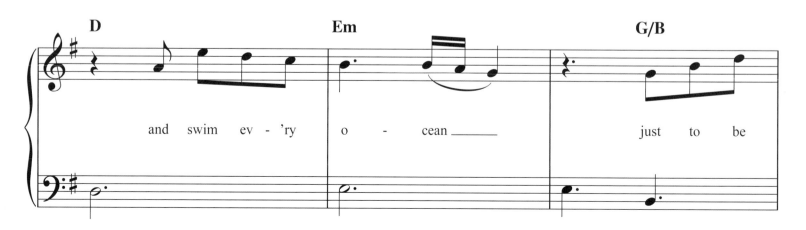

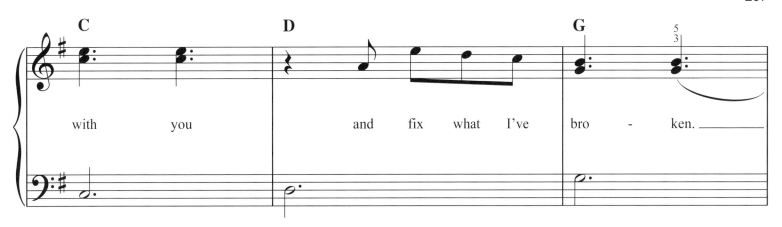

with you   and fix what I've bro - ken. _____

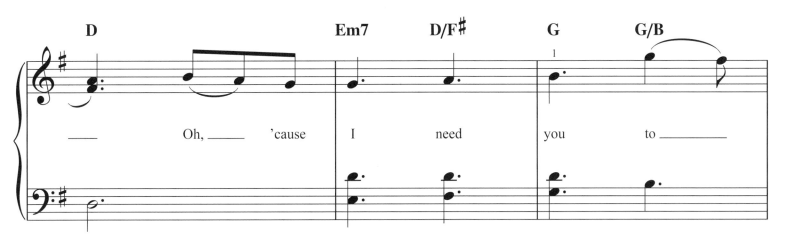

_____ Oh, _____ 'cause I need you to _____

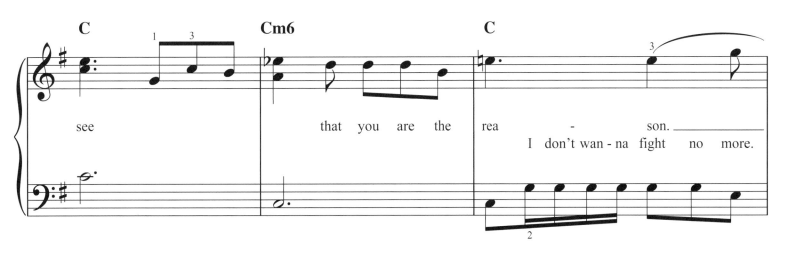

see   that you are the rea - son. _____

I don't wan - na fight no more.

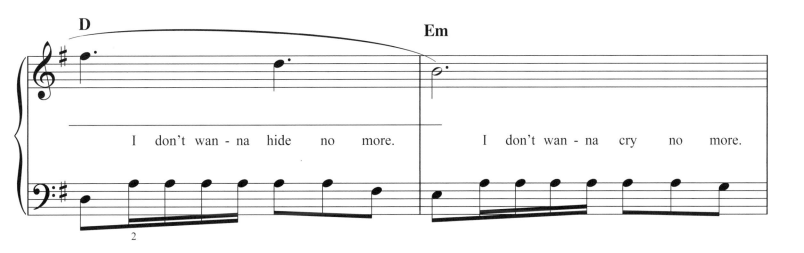

I don't wan - na hide no more.   I don't wan - na cry no more.

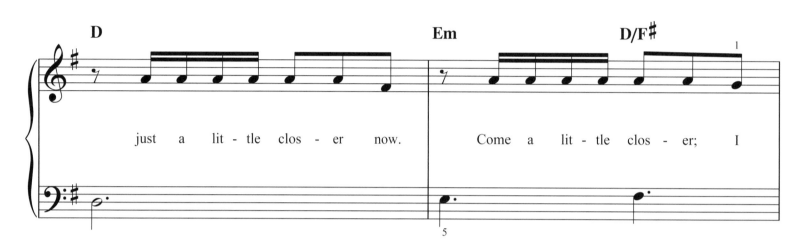

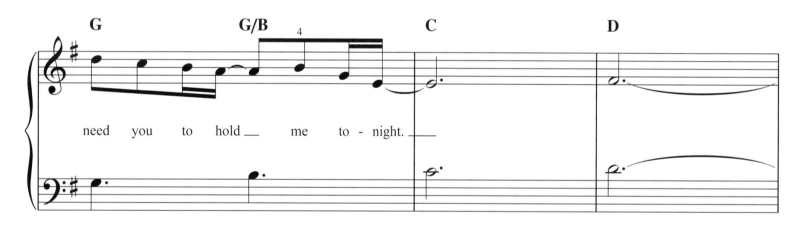

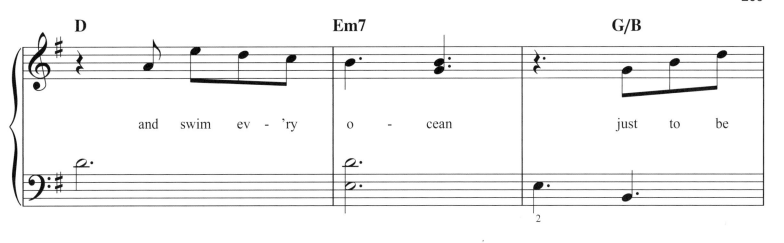

and swim ev - 'ry o - cean just to be

with you and fix what I've bro - ken.

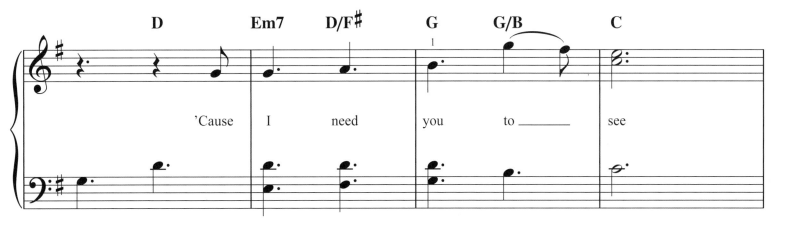

'Cause I need you to _____ see

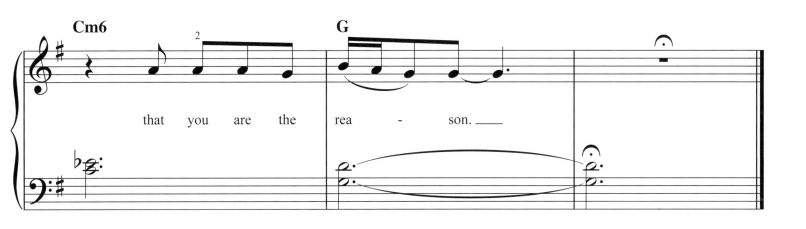

that you are the rea - son. _____

YOU HAD ME FROM HELLO

Words and Music by SKIP EWING
and KENNY CHESNEY

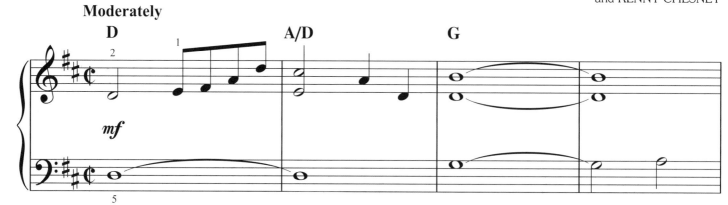

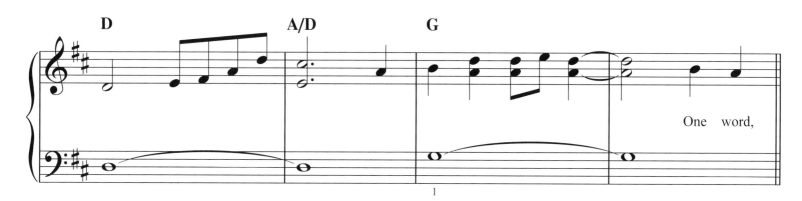

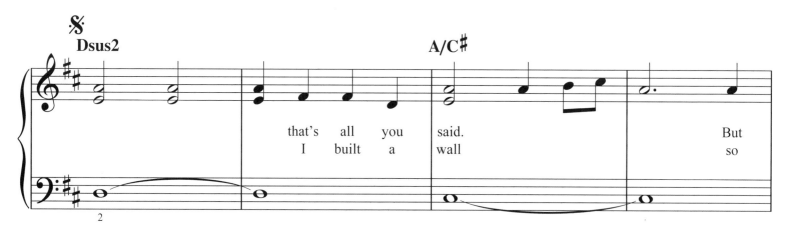

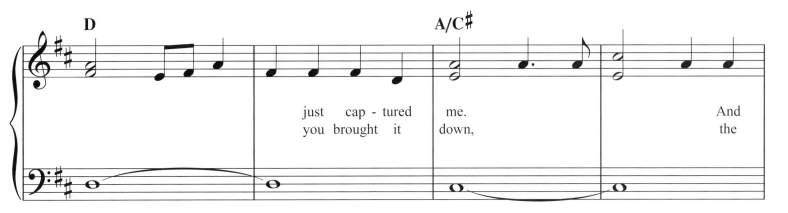

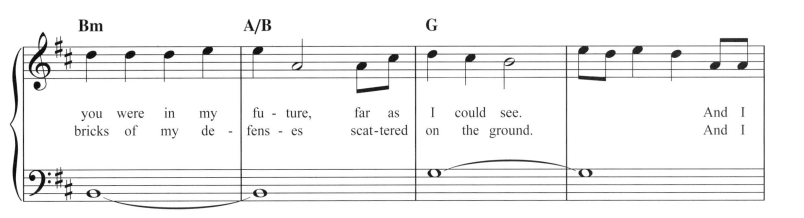

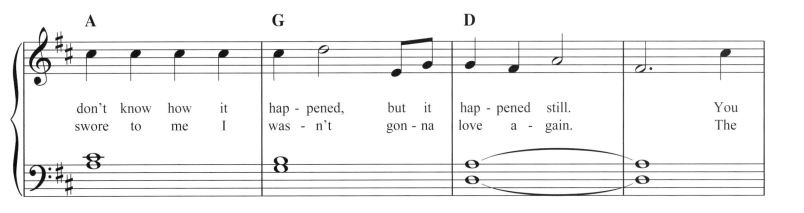

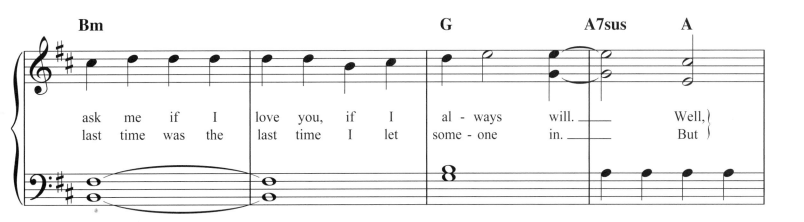

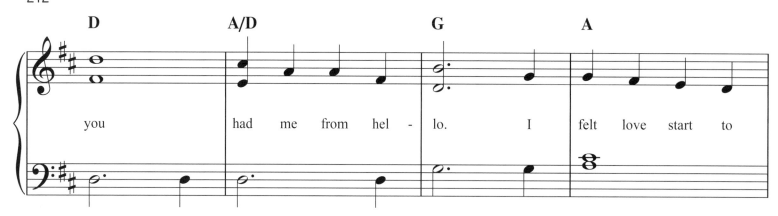

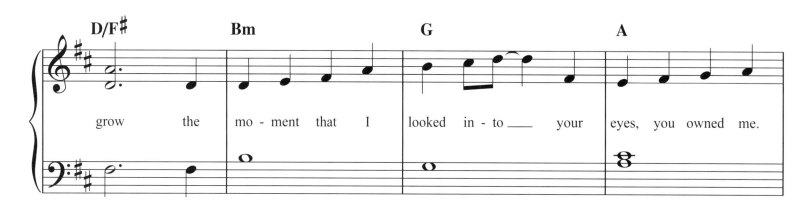

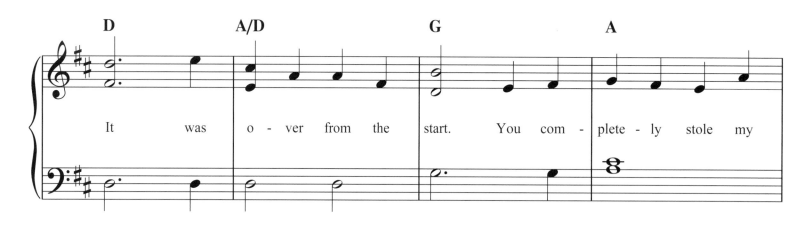

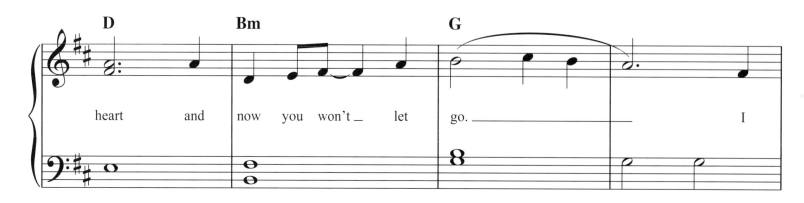

213

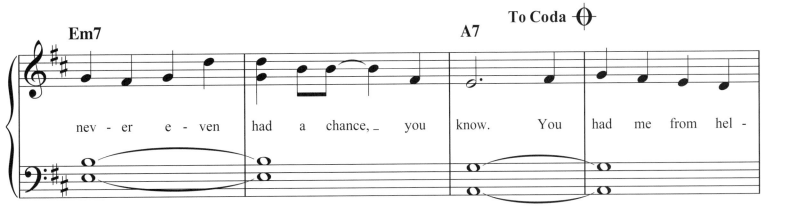

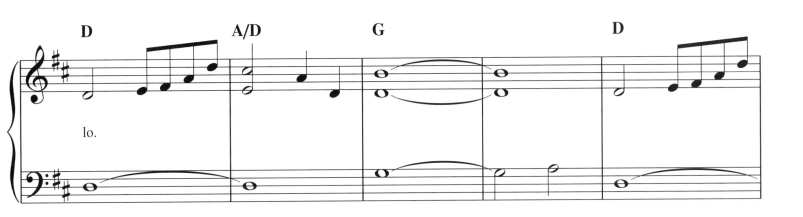

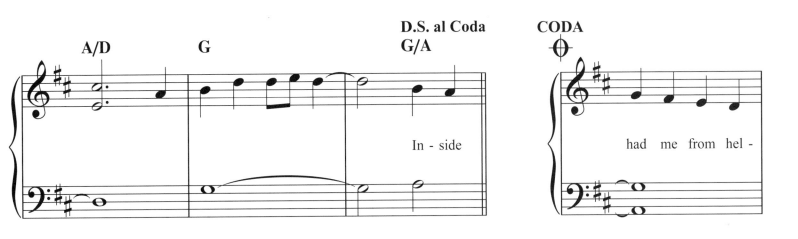

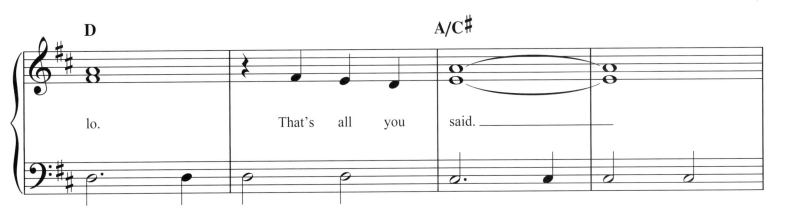

214

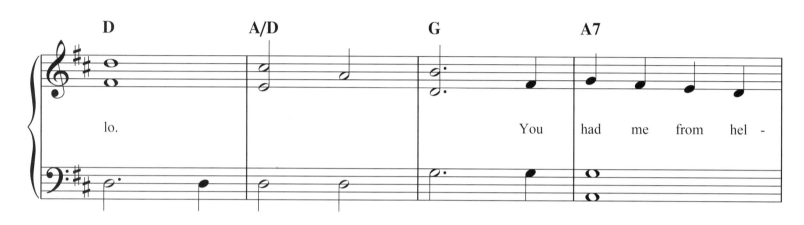

YOU MAKE MY DREAMS

Words and Music by SARA ALLEN,
DARYL HALL and JOHN OATES

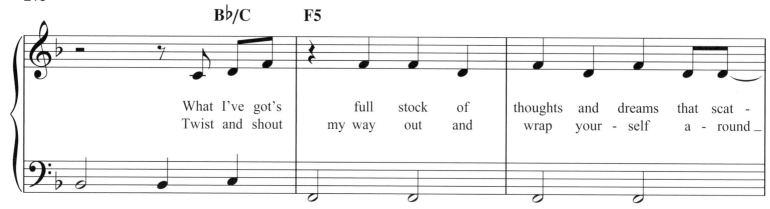

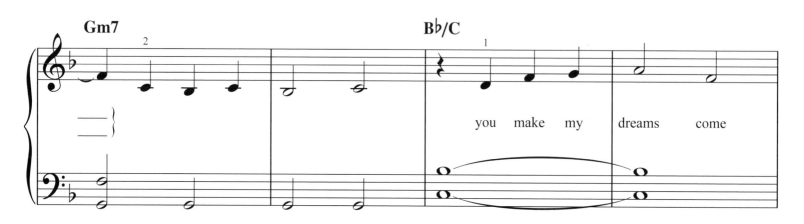

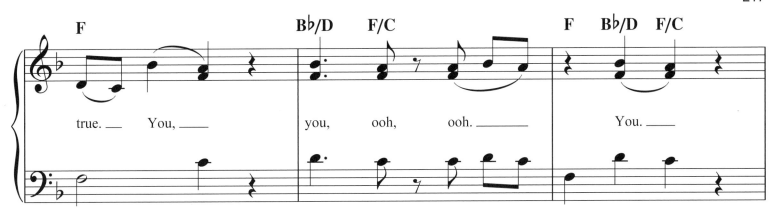

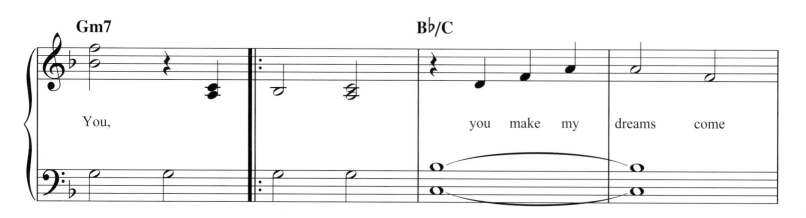

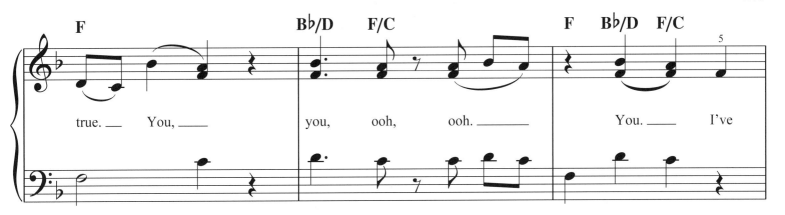

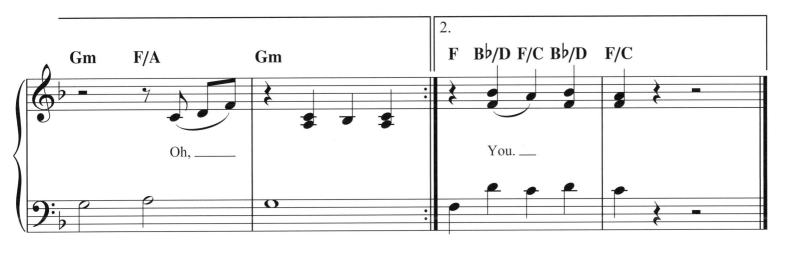

YOUR SONG

Words and Music by ELTON JOHN
and BERNIE TAUPIN

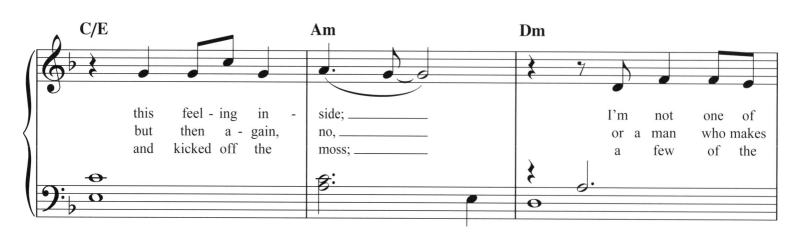

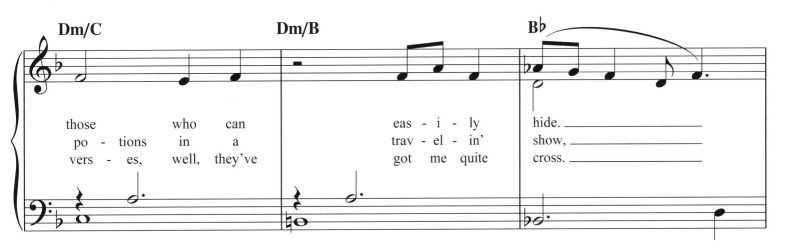

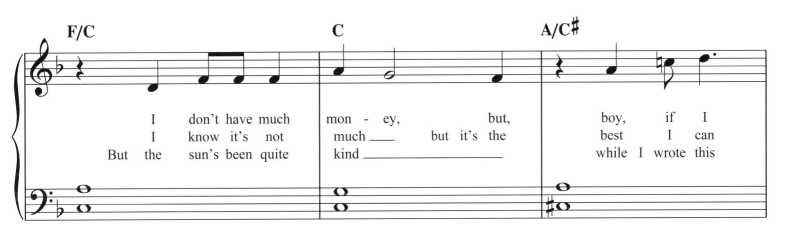

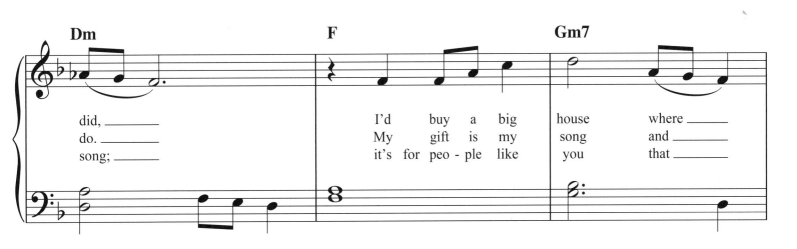

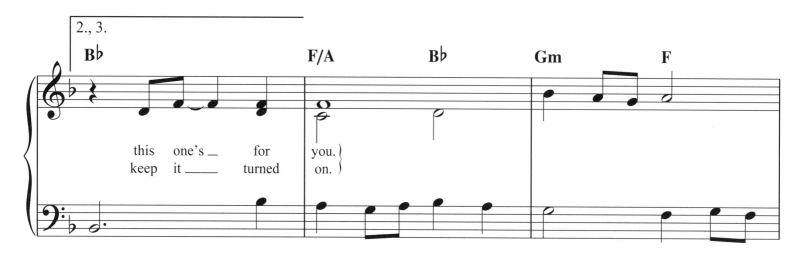

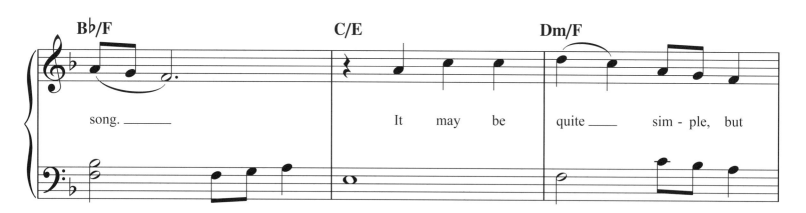

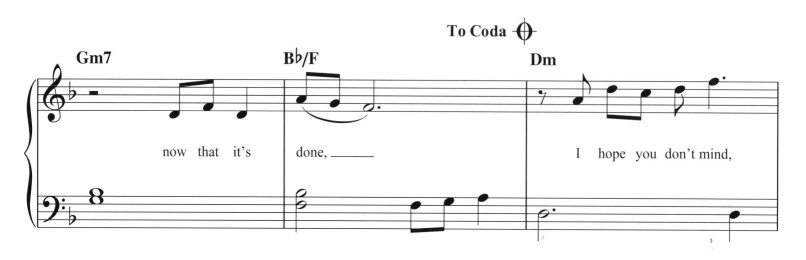

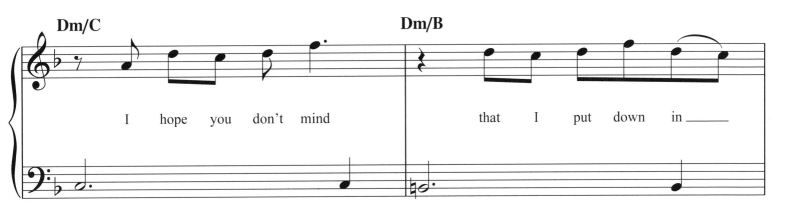

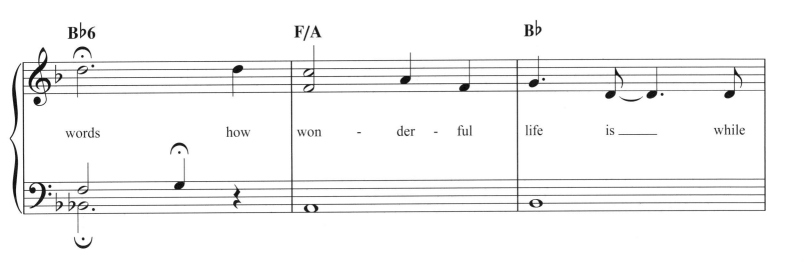

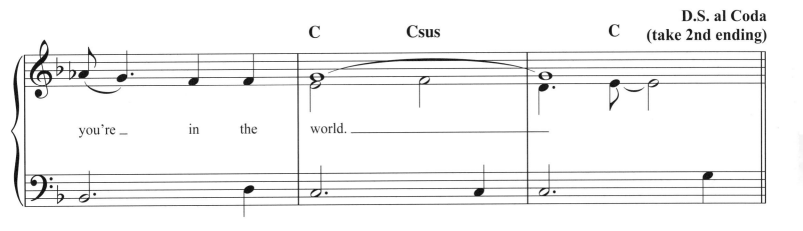

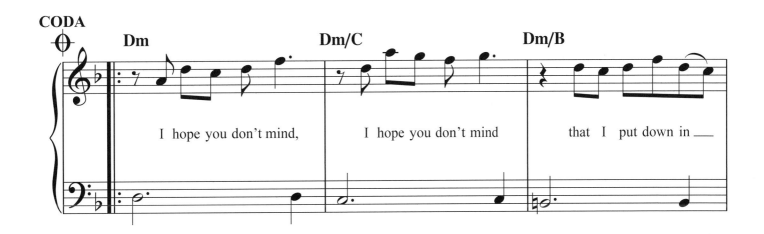

224

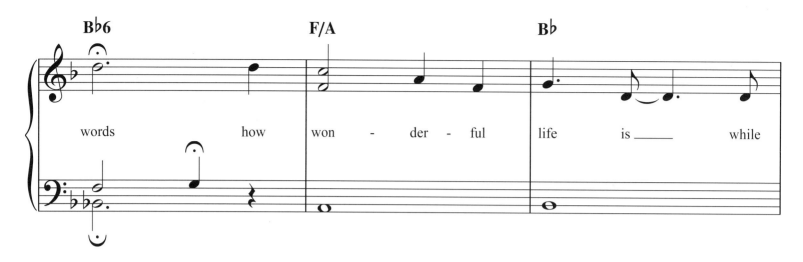

words   how   won - der - ful   life   is ____   while

you're _   in   the   world.

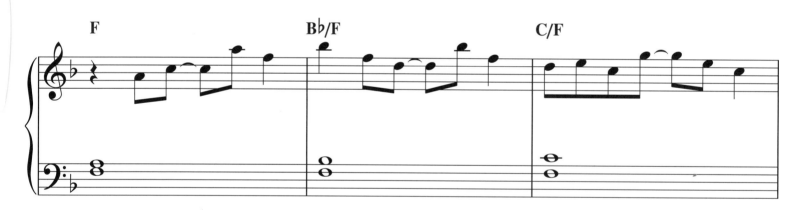

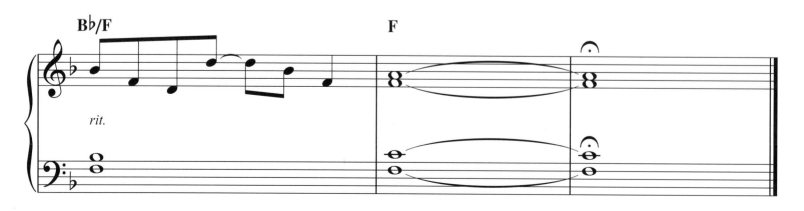

rit.